I HAVE *Nothing* to WEAR!

A Painless 12-Step Program
to Declutter Your Life So You
Never Have to Say This Again!

JILL MARTIN

and

DANA RAVICH

RODALE

Rodale books may be purchased for business or promotional use or for special sales. For information, please write to: Special Markets Department, Rodale, Inc., 733 Third Avenue, New York, NY 10017.

Printed in the United States of America
Rodale Inc. makes every effort to use acid-free ♾, recycled paper ♻.

Book design by Kara Plikaitis
Illustrations by Monica Lind

Library of Congress Cataloging-in-Publication Data

Martin, Jill.
   I have nothing to wear! : a painless 12-step program to declutter your life so you never have to say this again! / Jill Martin and Dana Ravich.
      p.   cm.
   ISBN 978–1–60529–077–5   hardback
   1. Clothes closets.   2. Storage in the home.   3. Beauty, Personal.   I. Ravich, Dana.   II. Title.
TX309.M394   2011
648'.8—dc22   2011009993

Distributed to the trade by Macmillan
2   4   6   8   10   9   7   5   3   1   hardcover

We inspire and enable people to improve their lives and the world around them.
www.rodalebooks.com

This book is dedicated to our families. Not only for all their love and support—which has been a constant ALWAYS—but for each of their idiosyncrasies when it comes to fashion and their closets. They have taught us their lessons—from the reasons to keep everything from childhood on, to the virtues of knowing what to get rid of and when!

Martin, Georgette, Jon, Robert, Lucy, Helen, Rachel, Lyle, Lou Lou, Leo.

We love you.

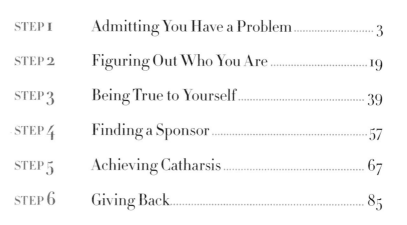

Contents

Breaking Down
Fashion
Confusion

Admitting You Have a Problem

3

Is your wardrobe a confusing mess? Do you go through the same grueling process every day when trying to pick an outfit? Do you have too many items in your closet—or all the wrong ones? Do many clothes still have the tags attached even though you didn't purchase them this week, or even this year? Do you shop just to lift your mood?

Let's go a step further. Most days do you find yourself in an outfit that is OK, but not great? Do you turn down evening invitations because you're not happy with the way you look and feel in your outfit, and don't have time to go home and change after work? Would a stop home help even if you did have time?

Do you lack the confidence to ask for that promotion, or even to speak up in a meeting?

Do you avoid eye contact with the hot guy in your building because you never feel like you look hot enough?

Are you always running late because you can never figure out what to wear? Does everything just spiral downward from there?

Have you, on more occasions than you care to admit, stood in front of an overstuffed closet saying, "I have nothing to wear!"

Have you, on more occasions than you care to admit, stood in front of an overstuffed closet saying, "I have nothing to wear!"

Well, if you answered "yes" to any or all of the above, the diagnosis is:

You have a dysfunctional wardrobe.

Now take a deep breath. Everything's going to be OK. Don't feel bad. You are in the vast majority. The good news is there is a cure. So go ahead, admit it! Once you realize that this is a real problem, you're on the way to fixing it. Yes, fixing it.

You know how different you feel on days you *throw* yourself together as opposed to the days you *put* yourself together. How you feel on the days you wear unflattering clothes because, for whatever reason, they are in your closet and will do, for work anyway, compared with those days you are in a dress that looks like it was made just for you, and you had your hair blown out to boot. Then there are those days that you can't wait to go home, crawl in bed, and hope for better tomorrow, as opposed to the days you never want to end and feel like you could dance all night.

Are most of your days the thrown-together, crawl-back-in-bed kind of days, rather than the hot-dress, dance-all-night days?

your closet is disorganized

Let's dive into your closet and see what's going on in there. We're envisioning shelves holding piles with no rhyme or reason. Pants are mixed with tops, T-shirts with sweaters. The colors are not grouped. Nothing is neatly folded. (You were rushing after you tried everything on in a last-minute panic.)

The rack is overstuffed. You can barely see what's hanging. Some dresses are mashed behind others. *Everything* is wrinkled. The pants are not hanging together, nor are the tops, skirts, or dresses. The clothes are all randomly put away, in no particular order, and not arranged by color or any system. Some pieces are even dangling by one end of the hanger. Sound familiar?

Allow us to continue. Your shoes are piled on the floor of your closet. No wonder it sometimes takes twenty minutes just to find the mate to the one you want to wear. And most of them aren't even comfortable.

How can your day possibly start off right if you have to contend with this mess every morning? We're exhausted just thinking about it!

Bags are shoved up high on a shelf. You can't see half of them, let alone reach them. Like your clothes, they are squished and crushed. This is probably not how you planned to treat that bag the day you happily carried it out of the store.

We're not even going to go into coats and jackets right now. We only hope they are in a separate closet.

Underwear, belts, jewelry. Please tell us these have a proper place. Right now, our best guess is that some belts are still in the pant loops, your jewelry is tangled together in a big pouch, and your underwear is all mixed up.

How can your day possibly start off right if you have to contend with this mess every morning? We're exhausted just thinking about it!

you have too much stuff

One reason your closet looks like this is that you are afraid to get rid of anything. You think maybe it'll come back in style. Or you don't have the time or energy to deal with all that stuff. Or your weight goes up and down. Or you love your college sweatshirts even if they are all XXL.

Jill

A few years ago, I bought a pair of Christian Louboutin stilettos. I *had* to have them. I was shopping at Saks, and when I tried them on, I said to myself, "I can't really walk in these, but that's OK, I will just be going from the taxi to dinner, and won't have to walk *that* far." (Can you say "rationalize"?) Those shoes sat in my closet for three years. Every time I got dressed up to go out, I thought about wearing them, but then quickly realized I didn't want to be uncomfortable and thought better of it. Finally I took them to a consignment shop. They sold them for me, and I made half of my money back! Some other woman is now walking around in my fab, must-have shoes, but I am comfortable and $275 richer!

Dana

I totally used to be "that girl." I always thought there might be an occasion when I would need something (even for a Halloween costume!) so I didn't want to get rid of it—just in case. I, too, held on to shoes that I never wore. One pair in particular was these beautiful turquoise, strappy, high-heeled Michel Perry sandals. Something was wrong with one strap when I bought them. I chose to ignore that fact, but every time I went to wear them, the offending shoe didn't stay on my foot properly, and I had to take them off before I even left the house. Finally, one day I realized that I was being ridiculous, and that no matter what I got rid of, I would still be able to find something in my closet to wear—no matter where I was going. And you know what? If I really needed something new, I would just get it when the time came. The reality is, I always have something to wear, even in my minimalist wardrobe.

You spent so much money on those pants. Your sweats are so soft and cozy, even though they have holes and stains. The T-shirts are still sort of white, so you can get away with them. The shoes are only a half-size too small, and you're not walking very far.

Some people would call this saving for a rainy day. Others would call this hoarding.

However you justify it, rationalize it, or sleep at night with it, having too much clothing is a problem. Don't worry—help is on the way.

Are you really going to fit into clothes you wore in high school? What if you saved just your favorite college sweatshirt, since it makes you happy? What if you let those expensive pants go, the ones that don't fit you well? The stained and ripped sweats and the yellowed T-shirts—really!

What if you had a sexy pair of stilettos that actually fit? Instead of all that

junk, what if your whole wardrobe reflected the fabulous you of today? Flattered your figure? Made you feel sexy and confident? What if your closet was organized so that finding an outfit was easy and even fun? How would your day be then? Your mood? Your life?

The truth is, the more you collect, keep, and yes, hoard, the less you will value each item. And the less closet space you'll have! When you keep adding without subtracting, you find yourself in a real closet situation. When you have too much, you can't possibly see everything you have, can't keep track of what you have, can't keep it in perfect condition, and can't easily find things!

What if your closet was organized so that finding an outfit was easy and even fun? How would your day be then? Your mood? Your life?

you have too many different styles

It's easy to accumulate too much when you don't know your own style. This leads to buying what the magazines say is trendy, what the salesgirl recommends, or what you don't already own just for the sake of having a miniskirt or a top in bright orange. Sound familiar?

It's easy to be overwhelmed by all the options in the stores and the constantly changing (and returning) trends. However, grown-ups need to know their own styles. If you haven't yet found yours, well, that explains your closet confusion!

It is very frustrating to follow trends that don't flatter you, speak to your personality, or allow you to express yourself. We want you to feel comfortable in your own skin and let the world see you at your best. Have the confidence to go get that new job. Be brave enough to go on that blind date. You deserve all those things. Don't let your dysfunctional wardrobe hold you back any longer!

A lot of factors will shape your style. Your personality, career, and lifestyle are all part of the mix. We'll explain them all and help you find your own personal style. For now, just understand that you are not shopping smartly when you don't know your style. You end up buying a bit of everything, in a wide range of colors, and shopping way too often. When you don't know your style, every new thing you bring into your wardrobe makes it harder to figure out what goes with what, further clutters your closet, and takes away the fun of getting dressed.

> We want you to feel comfortable in your own skin and let the world see you at your best.

there are clothes with the tags still on

Here's another sign of trouble in the closet. How much money are you wasting on clothing that you don't even wear? We're talking about clothes that still have the tags attached. Funny how there can be brand new clothes in the closet, and you can still exclaim, "I have nothing to wear!" Again, you are not alone, and again, this is not right.

In *Sex and the City,* Carrie realizes she has spent the equivalent of a down payment for an apartment on shoes! Wouldn't you rather have a fabulous and

(continued on page 16)

I love wearing white, and I love statement jewelry. These are part of my personal style. My clothes are classic, with the jewelry adding a little flair. If you bump into me in the street, day or night, I will likely be in something white with a bold necklace, bracelet, or ring. I like to be the girl "who wears white and fun jewelry." Decide what you like the most and go with it. There are so many serious things to worry about. Your wardrobe should not be one of them. Have fun!

Dana

I definitely have a bohemian vibe in my wardrobe, personality, and lifestyle. Over the years I have come to know who I am, and my wardrobe reflects that. I have found my favorite stores (Calypso and Tomas Maier) and I stick to shopping primarily there. Each time I add a new piece to my wardrobe (since it screams "me") I can create several new outfits. By being true to myself and my style, I know each new item will work with most of what's already in my closet. When I purchase something that isn't "me," it ends up sitting in the closet unworn because I don't know how to incorporate it. The truth is, this doesn't really happen anymore. Lessons learned!

functional wardrobe without spending a dime more than you need to, and have the money for the other fun things in your life?

If your closet is disorganized, you probably don't know half of what's in there—new items included. If you tend to hoard your clothing, you probably "save" new purchases for a special occasion—the one that hasn't happened since you bought the item two years ago.

If you have too many different styles going on, because you don't know your individual style, then you probably bought a lot of pieces that were "in" at the time, but didn't really flatter your figure, or were a color that wasn't "you," or just didn't fit your lifestyle. Whatever the reason, we need to fix this ASAP!

you shop to improve your mood

One last sign of a dysfunctional wardrobe: You shop to make yourself feel better. You just went through a breakup, you didn't get the promotion you were counting on, or your family is driving you nuts. Doesn't everybody run straight to the mall? This is not about them, but about *you*. It's time to admit you have a problem and decide that there are no more excuses.

Do you know what happens when you shop in a bad mood? You overspend. It feels good to spend money, and you think those trinkets are going to make you feel

Jill

I shop when I am depressed. I walk around a store and say things like, "I am going to wear this $350 dress when I go with my fabulous boyfriend to St. Barths for the weekend and we are walking alone on the beach." The dress in question is actually see-through, so my made-up scenario involves us being solo with no one else on the beach. I bought the dress two summers ago at Calypso. Mind you, I have not gone on that vacation yet, and that beautiful dress that I bought on a spending-while-depressed splurge just hangs in my closet. *The worst part?* Dana got it at the end of the summer for $49 on the sale rack. Did she ever wear it? No—but at least she got a great deal.

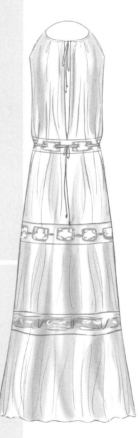

Dana

OK, admittedly, I haven't worn the dress yet either, but it is totally my vibe—and I will! I am more of a "shopping when I need something, want something, or find a great deal" girl than a mood shopper. So there tends to be a method to my madness. My purchases are pretty well thought out, which prevents the regret after the fact. We all know that lifting your mood is the worst reason to shop because the instant gratification is only that. Tempting as it may be, the purchase won't make you happy in the long run. And probably won't even keep you happy until the next day.

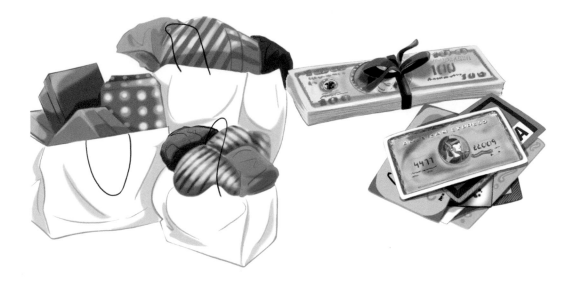

better. You buy things that you probably won't wear, because the bright color is making you happy in that moment. You might not even stop to try anything on. You just want it all. Who cares if it fits right? You'll worry about that later, even though the boutique doesn't accept returns. You aren't even thinking clearly about what you already have in your closet, so you end up with duplicates. Sound familiar?

Get ready to show the world your most fabulous self.

Are you ready to admit you have a problem? Yes? Remember, you aren't the only one in total fashion confusion.

Now get ready to let your fashion woes become history. You have taken the first step on the road. Get ready to show the world your most fabulous self. Get ready for people to see you the way you want them to. Get ready to start saying "yes"—to dinner, to a date, to a party. Get ready to change your life.

STEP 2

Figuring Out
Who You Are

You might be thinking, "I can skip this chapter.
I know who I am." You may be right, but your wardrobe isn't showing it. If it was,
you wouldn't be saying, "I have nothing to wear!"

Creating a wardrobe that reflects who you are takes more than knowing that
your favorite color is pink or that you work in
an office.

Let's break it down. Your personal style is
influenced by seven aspects of who you are:
your career, activities, marital and kid status,
where you live, age, body type, and, of course,
personality.

Your personal style is
influenced by your
career, activities, marital
and kid status, where you
live, age, body type, and,
of course, personality.

Jill

My life is nuts. Some days I start early in the morning on the *Today* show and end it late interviewing players in the Knicks' locker room. I need a wide variety of clothing to make it through the day, let alone a season. I dress up and look the part for everything my day entails, but this is my "thing": I do not wear my high heels until I get there! I know, I know: Heels make your legs look longer and make you look sexier. But I have to be honest with myself. I am much more comfortable in flats (I know many of you can relate). So, if you see me out and about, I will likely be in flats (still looking completely put together, of course) unless I am at the actual event or walking into it. I keep my heels in my purse and change in the car/taxi/ plane/train. All it takes is a little preparation. I believe being sexy is also about being comfortable. So while I own gorgeous stilettos, I only use them in minimal doses! Oh, and by the way, I don't *love* my legs, so skirts that hit above the knee are also out. Blanket rule.

Dana

O K, this has nothing to do with where I live, or whether or not I have kids, or even my body type, but there are definitely some things I've learned about myself when it comes to my wardrobe. I guess these would all fall in the personality category. I don't wear T-shirts, I don't wear belts, I don't wear silver jewelry, and I don't wear red. There, you have it. No reason, it's just who I am. The great thing about knowing all of this is that I just don't buy those things anymore. I used to, but I've learned. Those items will just end up sitting there. I will never reach for them, never wear them, and they will just end up having been a huge waste of money. So, you see, even when belts are all the rage, I sit that trend out. Believe me, there are plenty of ways for me to express my style without succumbing to every latest trend.

career

What kind of career do you have these days? Has it changed, and if so, is your style keeping up? Some full-time moms still have a closet cluttered with corporate suits.

Whether you are a lawyer, teacher, or someone in entertainment or fashion, you can still express yourself!

Please! We're not discouraging going back to work—in fact, quite the opposite. You should do whatever fulfills you and makes you happy. We're saying "please" because you think the suits you wore back in the day are still in style, still fit properly, and are still appropriate business attire!

Let's get real. What kind of career do you have? You spend most of your time at work, so your job, workplace, and industry will have a big impact on the wardrobe pieces you need in your closet.

At work you must dress within the parameters of your industry and office dress code while maintaining your style and identity. Whether you are a lawyer, teacher, or someone in entertainment or fashion, you can still express yourself!

If you work at a law firm, you probably have to wear a suit. If you are a schoolteacher, your dress will be more casual. If you work in the fashion or entertainment industry, you can (and probably need to) dress with more edge.

Whatever your career, getting dressed for work should be a no-brainer. You should not be peering into your closet every morning repeating, "I have nothing to wear!" Of course, some days you want to be more comfortable or dressier. The reason could be the weather, how well you slept, or plans after work. The goal is a closet with options for your varying moods.

However, whatever your mood, your job is the same. If you aren't a lawyer or

banker, why are all those suits taking up precious room in your closet? When you go shopping for work clothes, focus on what you will actually wear to work, so when you reach into your closet in the morning there will be no confusion or cause to run late.

activities

We hope that you don't spend all your time at work! What do you do in your free time? Do you like to shop and lunch with friends? Play tennis or golf? Go to the beach, yoga studio, gym? Play in the backyard with the kids? Curl up with a great book or your favorite magazines?

However you like to spend your time, you are going to need the right clothes. Yes, even for lounging at home. No matter what you are doing, and with whom, we want you to look your best. This does not mean always being decked out. It just means being in the best, most flattering, most appropriate, most personality-revealing outfit at any given moment.

If you enjoy lots of different activities, you'll need a variety of items in your wardrobe. That's perfectly acceptable. We're not saying get rid of everything you own. We're just saying get rid of everything you own that isn't working for you.

> No matter what you are doing, and with whom, we want you to look your best. This does not mean always being decked out. It just means being in the best, most flattering, most appropriate, most personality-revealing outfit at any given moment.

marital status/kids

Your wardrobe needs are also influenced by whether you are married or single and have kids or not. If you're chasing kids around the playground, you'll need different clothes than if you're chasing after the new "it" bag. We're not saying that you can't look cute, sexy, and stylish just because you have kids. In fact, we want you to look cute, sexy, and stylish with kids or without. If you wear flats instead of stilettos, or carry a big messenger tote instead of just a clutch, the items should still be flattering, in style, and put together.

Also, you need to look hot whether you're chasing after the hot single guy or are already married to your own hot guy. Being married is no excuse to wear any old thing in your closet. We know it takes effort to look your best all the time. Wouldn't it be easier if everything in your closet was already a great option? What if "any old thing" didn't even exist?

If you are single, then you should know that every moment counts—even running out for coffee in the morning. That's always when you run into "him," isn't it? The ex, the intriguing new guy in your building, or worse, the ex's new girlfriend.

Look your best for you! The way you put yourself together affects your mood, self-esteem, and attitude. So make it good.

We don't want you to look like you're trying too hard or overdressing. We just want you to look like the best you, and appropriate for the occasion.

By the way, the effort is not just for the man who is in your life (or the one

DO

DON'T

who's about to be). Look your best for you! The way you put yourself together affects your mood, self-esteem, and attitude. So make it good.

where you live

Also determining what you will need in your wardrobe is where you live. Are you a big-city girl living in a fashion capital like New York? Are you living somewhere more relaxed and casual, like the suburbs?

Where you live says a lot about who you are and what kind of wardrobe you need. If you are living in a city where people tend to dress up and are fashion savvy, you want a wardrobe to flourish in that environment, whether you are in the workplace, at restaurants or social gatherings, or even walking down the street. While you don't want to look like a carbon copy of everyone else, you do want to look the part.

Likewise, if you live in a suburb or small town, a certain look is right for the environment. Just because people dress more casually outside the big city is not a license to dress like a slob. Nor does it mean that you can't dress up. If you are a full-on fashionista living far from the fast lane, work it. You can still have fun with

No one wants to be a fashion victim, regardless of where she lives. Just keep it tame and take into account your surroundings.

the latest trends. Just try to keep it reasonable. No one wants to be a fashion victim, regardless of where she lives. Just keep it tame and take into account your surroundings. No matter where you live, remember to put your best self forward and express your personal style!

age

OK, this can be a tough one to incorporate into your style. Certain looks are more appropriate for women of a particular age, but there are women who defy age. Plenty of women are fifty and fabulous. They still have great legs or a great stomach. (But no stomach-baring tops, no matter how old you are or how flat your stomach!)

So how does age come into personal style? If you have great legs, show them off! Yes, you can wear a skirt above the knee after thirty—just don't try to wear a micro-mini like a teenager. Keep it tasteful. If you are fifty and fabulous, wear a skirt that hits just above the knee. If you are in your twenties and fabulous and want to go shorter, go for it!

There is room for everyone to express herself, show off her style, and play with trends.

All trends are available in a range of degrees. Clothing appropriate for the younger set will be more embellished, brighter, shorter, and more sheer—more extreme and obvious all around. While you may be able to push the envelope at a younger age, when you get a bit older you want a tamer version.

There is room for everyone to express herself, show off her style, and play with trends. In fact, over time you'll become even more confident about making trends work for you, since you will know who you are and what works on you. (If you don't know yet, keep reading!)

Jill

When I am not on the air or doing an interview, 99 percent of the time you will see me in workout clothing. This does not mean I am in an oversize sweatshirt and sweatpants. I make sure, even when dressed casually, that I am put together. My "uniform" consists of Lululemon (my favorite workout clothing brand) pants in black, a tight T-shirt, a cute pullover sweatshirt, and flip-flops. Dana and I use the same test for whether we look put together and appropriate before walking out the door: If I ran into my ex-boyfriend who broke my heart (we hate him now), would I be OK in this?

Dana

O K, I live in New York City, and I am the first to admit that I do not walk around all the time looking like a full-blown fashionista. Not even half the time. But, just like Jill, I am always put together, even when I'm just going to yoga in my I Am Beyond leggings, white tank, fitted jean jacket, small messenger-style bag, and flip-flops. Everything fits, looks cute, and expresses my personality, no matter where I am going, what I am doing, and whom I am with. Even if I do run into "him" on the street, I am happy and excited to have the encounter, not ducking and running as fast as I can in the opposite direction. It's a whole other story when you look great and feel great. It changes your attitude and boosts your confidence.

body type

Body type is another consideration when figuring out what should be in your wardrobe. Do you have a long or short waist? What's your shape? Are you plus size? Petite?

All items in your wardrobe should flatter your body type. We know you love the print of that blouse, but if the cut is not right for your shape, it shouldn't be in your closet.

Too often we buy clothes because we like the way they look on the hanger in the store, on the model in a magazine, or on a best friend. But everything doesn't look good on everybody. There, we said it. However, everybody can look good, or better yet, great! With some careful study of your figure, you'll figure out what's flattering (more on this to come).

> We know you love the print of that blouse, but if the cut is not right for your shape, it shouldn't be in your closet.

personality

Last but most important is your personality. Your wardrobe expresses your personality to the world. Your style tells people who you are, or at least introduces you.

Your personality has many facets. Are you fun, loud, quiet, shy, conservative, funky? Think about who you are, and then we can figure out your look.

By the way, a "look" does not mean you will wear the same thing day in and day out. It just means the overall vibe that works for you. Once you figure this out, you will be amazed how easy it is to figure out what to wear, no matter the occasion.

When your clothes reflect your personality, they can overlap from work to play. Not every item, obviously, but the overall look.

Wherever you work and live, whatever your age or body type, there's no excuse not to look your best even if you work in a corporate environment, spend most of your time chauffeuring kids, live in a small town, aren't twenty-five, have been married for years, or don't have the body of a model in *Vogue*. No matter what you're doing or where you go, look like "you"—the best "you." Let's go on.

Wherever you work and live, whatever your age or body type, there's no excuse not to look your best.

STEP

Being True to Yourself

It's time to figure out how *you* want to dress. In this
step, we will help you figure out, and be true to, your personal style.

A big reason you've been having trouble coordinating outfits is that your
closet has too many style options. We totally understand how it got that way. It's
very easy to get pulled in a million directions. You're looking through magazines,
watching what celebrities are wearing, listening to the salespeople at a variety of

shops. All the advice on what to wear and how to wear it can get very confusing, which leads to frustration, which leads to fashion overload, which inevitably leads to "I have nothing to wear!"

In step 2, you looked at yourself from a style point of view. It's time to connect what you learned about yourself to some style categories.

The six styles are classic girl, bohemian girl, preppy girl, fashionista, surfer chick, and soccer mom.

We are going to define six basic styles from which you will choose for yourself. There are no wrong choices.

The categories simplify styles so you can get a handle on shopping, dressing, and expressing yourself to the world. This doesn't mean you can never dress in clothes that are not the style you picked. But usually, you should. Knowing your style will streamline your choices so that it's easy to mix, match, and let your personality shine.

The six styles are classic girl, bohemian girl, preppy girl, fashionista, surfer chick, and soccer mom. Each style has a trademark look, color scheme, and vibe. Each speaks volumes about the woman who wears it.

classic girl

The classic girl's closet is filled with basics that will stand the test of time. If you were to spot her on the street she would be wearing a white button-down shirt tucked into dark denim jeans. She'd wear a leather belt (with a gold or silver buckle), a structured medium-size purse, and ballet flats—all in a matching neutral, either black or tan. She might be wearing big black Jackie O. sunglasses and have a printed silk scarf around her neck or tied to her purse.

CLASSIC GIRL

A scarf provides a dose of color in the classic girl's wardrobe, which is mostly solid and neutral in color. Navy, white, black, and tan make up her palette.

If she's dressing up to go out for dinner, she'll swap the shoes and bag for a pair of high-heeled pumps and a clutch. She might also lose the silk scarf and add a fitted black blazer.

She will almost always wear a pair of diamond stud earrings and a watch, either an oversize metal one or one with a black leather strap.

Her look is easy, chic, and, well, classic. It will never go out of style.

This style works in both the city and the suburbs. It can work in an office and it can work if you are a stay-at-home mom. This look works at any age and for every body type. It exudes strength. The classic girl looks put together. Like she has her act together. She is organized and she can multitask.

The question is whether the style works for you. If so, everything must be of high quality and look impeccable. Clothes must fit and flatter, and be in perfect condition.

> Her look is easy, chic, and, well, classic. It will never go out of style.

bohemian girl

At the other end of the style spectrum is the bohemian girl. While the classic girl's clothes and accessories are structured, the bohemian girl's look is softer and more flowing. A typical outfit might be boyfriend or flared-leg jeans and a peasant top with gladiator sandals and a slouchy oversize hobo bag.

Even though this is a very different look than the classic girl's wardrobe,

BOHEMIAN GIRL

these pieces can be just as timeless. The look first became popular in the sixties and is still going strong. Sometimes hippie chic is trendier than other times, but the general vibe continues. Bohemian is more an attitude and an expression of personality than a fashion trend. Attitudes and personalities don't change with every "it" bag.

The bohemian girl also keeps it neutral in the color department. White is one of her faves, along with denim, metallic, and anything in the tan/brown family.

Her jewelry tends to look earthy and natural, perhaps an armful of gold bangles and long delicate chains around her neck. Maybe some freshwater pearls.

This look is soft and romantic and expresses a carefree attitude. It can work anywhere, but definitely says, "I wish I was in out in a beautiful field somewhere."

This woman might be a mom (very earthy) or she might have a career, or both. Chances are good she works in a creative industry.

The look skews youthful, but we know plenty of women of all ages who carry it off. Like we said, it's an attitude. Is it yours?

> Bohemian is more an attitude and an expression of personality than a fashion trend. Attitudes and personalities don't change with every "it" bag.

preppy girl

Preppy has the structured feel of the classic style, but is more casual and louder! It's funny that, even though preppy clothes are colorful and patterned, preppy girls are thought of as old-school and conservative. This look is associated with weekends at the country club, although it works way past the tennis court.

PREPPY GIRL

The preppy girl might wear a pink polo shirt with white jeans, a ribbon belt, Jack Rogers sandals, and a canvas boat tote.

Any color goes, but most popular are pink, kelly green, and navy blue. Colors are mixed and matched with each other and with neutrals like khaki and white. Madras, seersucker, and cable knit are preppy staples. Perhaps she's wearing madras print Bermuda shorts and a cable knit sweater.

Her jewelry is in keeping with her vibe. Pearl stud earrings are her everyday wear. She will also have a pearl necklace and a diamond tennis bracelet or two.

While the preppy girl might have a career and live in the big city, she is most closely associated with the suburbs and a life that revolves around family and activities. She is probably involved in her community and volunteer work.

It is common to see whole families dressed in preppy style. The preppy look is multigenerational and definitely defies age constraints.

Since this look is known for color and pattern, the preppy girl needs to make sure a print is flattering to her figure. If you are trying to make your bottom appear leaner, wear the print on top. If you're trying to minimize your waist or upper body, wear the print on the bottom.

But first ask yourself, "Is this look me?" Preppy style speaks to a very specific personality and lifestyle. If it is calling to you, embrace it. If not, keep looking.

fashionista

The fashionista really loves to dress in the latest trends and strut her style. A fashionista is a woman who knows her body, knows what works on her. She knows the trends and knows how to wear them to her advantage. She is in no way, shape, or

FASHIONISTA

form a fashion victim. Even though she loves being current and in the know, she does not succumb to every trend just because she saw it in *Vogue.*

This is definitely a big-city girl, or one at heart. She could live anywhere, but she'll probably gravitate to a fashion capital like New York City. The opportunity to shop and browse in actual stores as opposed to online is just too big a draw.

She is most likely a career woman. She needs to keep herself in all the latest and greatest, and she earns enough to do that. She might have a high-powered job in entertainment or even law. She definitely means business. She also loves attending parties and events.

Age is not a factor. Fashionistas are diehards. Once a fashionista, always a fashionista.

She might be married or not. Have kids or not. Either way, she's got it covered. Strong, like the classic girl, she is put together and has her act together. She knows how to work it.

Age is not a factor. Fashionistas are diehards. Once a fashionista, always a fashionista.

She puts together her look from a variety of trends. She might wear skinny jeans or high-waisted jeans. She might wear a pencil skirt or a miniskirt. She might wear a ruffled blouse or a cool blazer with a bit of color. She will most likely be in high heels. These might be stilettos or wedges. She will be current, but she will make the best choice for her figure.

She will always be chic, and she will almost always be dressed in black. Even though she is always on trend, her look won't vary that much, since she incorporates only what works for her. She makes subtle adjustments. When the toe shape changes from pointy to round, her shoes change. When purse size changes from large to small, her bag changes. When larger costume jewelry is in, she might incorporate that. She follows the trends and makes them work for her. She's a pro. Are you?

surfer chick

If you feel most at home on the beach or a mountain slope, perhaps you are a surfer chick.

You don't have to actually surf to be a surfer chick, but you're probably athletic and love being outdoors. You love the *idea* of surfing and that whole culture.

The typical surfer chick works to live and lives to surf. In other words, surfing (or skiing or snowboarding or hiking or pretty much anything outdoors) comes first, and everything else must be scheduled to accommodate the rising tide or the fresh powder. Including her job.

Much like the preppy type, a surfer chick can be any age. She might be married with little surfer babies, or her family might be everyone out on the swell. This is a culture, a lifestyle, not a hobby.

Being in top shape comes with the territory. To stand out in the ocean or the powder, she wears bright colors. No wallflowers in this crowd.

She still needs to pick clothes that flatter her figure. So whether she's in a bikini and a rash guard, or totally geared up in layers of ski clothes, she needs to choose wisely.

If it were up to her, all she would need in the shoe department are Ugg boots and flip-flops.

SURFER CHICK

Her jewelry is also minimal. Nothing that gets in the way, just a cool, chunky silver ring or cuff bracelet if she's dressing up.

Sound like paradise to you?

soccer mom

Maybe you'd rather let your kids do the running around while you root from the bleachers. Of course, if you're a soccer mom, your whole life is kind of a workout!

This girl needs a break. But whether she's chauffeuring carpool, running errands, or trying to get dinner on the table, she still must look and feel like a 10. Married with kids is no excuse to get lazy in that department.

However, she needs functional, comfortable clothes. Maybe she's wearing jeans (whatever style most flatters her figure), a cute V-neck top or sweater, ballet flats (of course), and a bag big enough to tote all she and the kids will need for the day.

Her wardrobe is made up of solids and darker colors. It doesn't have to be, but she likes to keep it simple. It takes less time to coordinate her outfit, and spills and stains don't show as much.

If she is going out at night, she will change out of the stained clothes, of course. Possibly into a dressier top, jeans, and perhaps heels if she's in the mood. Since she won't need all the kid stuff, she will grab a smaller purse. Still keeping it simple and easy, but sexy to remind herself she's a woman.

Depending on how old her kids are, she might wear some fine jewelry. Too much gets in the way and the little kids are always grabbing at it.

While being a soccer mom used to mean the suburbs, these days a fair share

(continued on page 55)

Jill

I am a classic girl at heart, but I certainly dabble in the fashionista world. If you were to ask me my everyday uniform, it would be a white T-shirt, jeans, ballet flats, and a chic bag. I have mostly black, white, ivory, and navy in my closet. (I have to wear a variety of different colors on television, so I have those options too. If not for that, my wardrobe would look pretty plain.) I like it that way. My fashionista side comes out through my jewelry. If you were to ask colleagues or friends of mine, "What is the one thing that Jill wears that stands out?" they would say statement jewelry. I use it to express my personality. Sometimes I try to go into other fashion worlds, but most of the time it doesn't work. My friend Alison, who owns a store called 25 Park, was wearing this fabulous loose bohemian dress. I loved it. She said, "I have it at my store, go get it." So of course I had to have it, and immediately ran to try it on. It looked ridiculous on me. Sometimes I wish I could pull off that look, but it is just not me. I am a classic fashionista and I am proud of it!

Dana

I am definitely a bohemian girl (with a bit of fashionista in the mix). No matter where I'm going, my vibe is pretty much that. Don't get me wrong. If the occasion is dressy, I will be dressy. If the situation is conservative, I can be that, too. However, regardless of the location or the circumstances, I will still be me. That means even if I'm wearing a white button-down shirt, it's soft, not stiff and structured or crisp. All my clothes work together because every time I add a new piece, I stay true to my style. Mostly you'll find me in jeans and a soft, unstructured top or a flowing, feminine dress. I'm almost always in flats, sandals, or boots. I generally carry an unstructured hobo bag. And my signature jewelry is layered delicate gold chain necklaces with charms (by Lizzie Scheck) and my collection of gold bracelets, some with beads and some bangles. That is my bohemian side. I have a bit of fashionista in me, too. When the fashionista mood strikes, my dress is more sophisticated, edgier. I wear something black, or more structured, or trendy (but only if it works for me). I put on my high heels, and I love a fun cocktail ring. Of course over the years I have tried out some other styles. I have been preppy at times, and classic at times. But years ago, I hit my stride, figured out my style, and it has been working for me ever since. Because I know who I am and what works on me, I am able to minimize what's in my closet, save money, and never utter the words, "I have nothing to wear!"

SOCCER MOM

choose to stay in the city. Keeping the look pretty basic works in either locale. Does it work for you?

Finding your style is an exercise in finding who you are. What do you want the world to see? No matter what your career, age, body type, marital status, or location, your personality needs to shine through, and your clothing needs to accommodate your lifestyle and make you feel like your best self. A perfect 10.

Finding a Sponsor

You have a lot to think about, and we've only just begun! Take a deep breath. This whole process may seem daunting, but we really want you to stick with the program. You will be so glad you did.

Uncluttering your closet (and your life) is going to take some work, but think of this as an adventure. Won't it be more fun if you take a friend along?

> This whole process may seem daunting, but we really want you to stick with the program. You will be so glad you did.

enlist a trusted friend

In this step, find a trusted friend to help you on your journey. Someone who has your best interests at heart, will be brutally honest, and has good taste. These qualities are all very and equally important. This person will become your "sponsor."

Of course, we will be your friends throughout the process, too, but you need someone there to psychologically hold your hand. Those of you who think you can be your own sponsor, remember we all need a little help from our friends. Would you be reading this book if you were handling things so well all on your own? We thought not.

The sponsor could be your best friend, a sibling, or a co-worker. Guy or girl. As long as he or she fits the requirements below, you're good to go. (But don't pick your mother. Odds are she'll be your biggest fan or worst critic. Either way, her vision can be clouded, and her advice not always spot-on.)

When deciding whom to pick as your sponsor, ask these questions:

- Are you comfortable with this person? No-holds-barred comfortable? Remember, you will be showing this person your very best and very worst. The sponsor will see every single item in your closet.
- Is this person honest? This person is going to be giving thumbs up or thumbs down on every item in your closet. Do you trust that he/she will be brutally honest and not spare your feelings?
- Does this person have style? Do you respect this person's opinion on what to keep and what to unload?
- Is this person familiar with your lifestyle?
- Does he or she know your personality?
- Does this person understand your body type and will he or she be honest enough to tell you what flatters and what makes you look a little less than your best self?

- Can you laugh and have fun with this person? Please choose someone with whom you can. This process is a million times better if you can laugh your way through it!

honest, ruthless

It's very important to pick someone who will be honest and ruthless with you. You certainly don't want someone telling you everything looks great and that someday, somewhere, you might wear it.

Your sponsor needs to be take-no-prisoners ruthless about your clothes. Clearly you've been hanging on to most of the garments in your closet for the wrong reasons. Maybe you don't know what's in your closet, maybe you're kind of a hoarder, maybe you don't know your style, maybe some pieces still have tags on and how can you get rid of something if it's brand new, or maybe it made you so happy the day you bought it, really cheered you up out of that foul mood. Really, we do get it. But now it's time for you to get it. These are not reasons. These are excuses.

The sponsor cannot be afraid to be real, honest, and strong with you. Your sponsor must be decisive, clear, and opinionated. And you must listen.

> The sponsor cannot be afraid to be real, honest, and strong with you. Your sponsor must be decisive, clear, and opinionated. And you must listen.

Of course, some items will be debated during your wardrobe assessment sessions, or "rounds" as we like to call them. Toss these into a "maybe" pile, keep going, and come back to them at the end. As you do this more often, and after you've laughed your way through most of your closet, you'll see that the "maybes" are really "nos" and you will be more inclined to let them go. Baby steps are OK.

When we describe your sponsor as ruthless, we mean it as a compliment. This person should be able to look at your clothes, look at you in your clothes, and call it: yea or nay. Your sponsor has no emotional attachment to your clothing, is assessing the fit with a fresh and objective eye, and hopefully knows you and current fashions enough to discern what you will and won't wear again.

Your sponsor has to be bold enough to tell you what is worth keeping and what goes straight to the toss pile (more later on where the toss pile goes).

take stock

Invite your friend to preview your closet and see what's in store. No judgments. We understand the shame, embarrassment, and hesitation, but truly yours isn't the worst closet out there. It certainly isn't the first to need help, nor will it be the last. Be proud you are getting help. That's more than most can say.

Jill

I am very good at telling other people what works and looks good on them. Every Friday, on the *Today* show's Ambush Makeover, Louis Licari and I pluck two women from Rockefeller Plaza and take them from frumpy to fabulous. I am constantly dealing with different body types and different tastes, but I always know what works and what doesn't. What is amazing is that when it comes to *me,* I am totally off! When I was working in Los Angeles a couple of months ago, I went into a very trendy boutique and picked out a dress. It was pale pink with a sweetheart neck and pockets. (I love anything with pockets.) Anyway, I thought it was stunning, sexy, and sophisticated, and I planned on wearing it out that same night to meet someone I was interested in. Apparently I was wrong. My friend Lyndsey was with me when I was getting ready. I put the dress on, and she said, "*That* is what you are wearing? It looks like a muumuu!" The fact is I am off all the time. Dana is my official sponsor. Every few months, she sits on my bed and I try on different items. About 90 percent of the time she tells me to ditch it. I'm lucky to have her.

Dana

OK, OK, I admit it! Even my closet has items that shouldn't be in there. I know, I know. Horrible. And I have nothing! I pride myself on being a minimalist, and I am not attached to most things material in nature. But even though I'm not hoarding things just because I don't want to let them go, sometimes even I don't notice everything in my closet. Some stuff just remains there inexplicably, even when it shouldn't. To remedy this, every once in awhile (or whenever I'm in the mood), I'll do a "round." I look for pieces that have been in my closet, but are not my go-to pieces, and I make an executive decision to let them go. I haven't worn them in ages, so I'll just get rid of them, for whatever reason—I don't like the way they look on me anymore, I don't like the material, or I just replaced them with something better. So, you see, this closet project really is a work in progress and we can all do better.

Some people have many closets and some have one overstuffed closet. The common denominator is that most don't know what's going on in their closet(s).

You can't fix your entire closet in one pass, so you need to take a staged approach to weeding out what doesn't work. We call each one of these passes a "round." If your closet is a total mess, it's going to take a few rounds to straighten it out.

On each round, you will go through every item of clothing and decide whether it is worthy enough to stay in your closet or should go in the toss pile (to sell, donate, or give away). You can also create a "maybe" pile. The maybe pile is actually a holding place, but makes it easier to give things up; you know it really should be tossed, and you'll get there next round.

We understand the shame, embarrassment, and hesitation, but truly yours isn't the worst closet out there. It certainly isn't the first to need help, nor will it be the last. Be proud you are getting help. That's more than most can say.

It's hard for some people to be ruthless enough on the first go-round, which is one of the reasons why there are "rounds" plural!

We recommend that your sponsor be there because you need an objective opinion on fit, look, and style. You may also need a little extra push to part with certain things. Having company also makes the process fun, rather than a chore you are stuck doing home alone.

Be realistic when you approach your closet with your sponsor. Figure out a plan of attack that works for both of you.

- Time of day Perhaps you like to try on clothes first thing in the morning, before you've eaten anything heavy, while you feel thinnest and most comfortable. Perhaps you would rather open up a bottle of wine and do this in the evening. Either way, make sure you both have your wits about you—you're not too starving to focus and you're not too tipsy to care!

- Pacing yourselves Chances are good that you will not be able to get through your entire wardrobe in one sitting. Give every item the attention it deserves. You don't want to keep things you don't need, or put a really great piece in the toss pile. This is going to take some time, so sit together with your calendars and book a few time slots so that you commit to seeing the project through.

- Make it fun If you choose to do a morning round, plan to go work out or have brunch, or both, afterward. If you do it at night, take your sponsor to dinner or a movie, or just chill and finish the bottle of wine.

your *Sex and the City* moment

In *Sex and the City,* the girls get together to clean out Carrie's closet because she is finally moving in with Big. If you don't remember the scene, or haven't seen the movie, we highly recommend renting it with your sponsor. Not only will the entire movie inspire you with all of the fabulous fashion, but the closet clean-out scene will show you how hilarious it can be to go through your entire wardrobe and take stock—honest stock.

Carrie tries everything on for her team of sponsors as they hang out and sip champagne, but your first round does not even require trying things on. First, plenty of items will go straight into the toss pile for reasons far more urgent than fit. (And you know those pieces are in there!)

Sorting without trying on is a better way to start. You ease into the process without worrying about body issues, and your sponsor will feel more comfortable being objective when garments are not attached to your body.

Once you have your sponsor ready to go, and you've scheduled at least two or three rounds in your calendar, you're almost ready to get started. Don't worry, we'll tell you how to work the rounds. We won't leave you to fend for yourself in the big bad forest that is your closet!

STEP 5

Achieving Catharsis

Now that you have your sponsor, it's time to clean out the closet! Don't panic. This is going to be fun. *Really!* Don't worry, we won't haphazardly, randomly take away all your favorite things. Trust us.

is it a 10?

In an organized and methodical way, you will decide what to keep and what to get rid of.

We want you to always look your very best. Whether you are running out for the paper, going to the gym, or attending a black tie affair, you should look like a 10, best on a scale of 1 to 10.

What defines a 10?

- Flatters your figure
- Shows your personality

(continued on page 70)

Jill

I am going to share a moment I would rather forget. I was going to an event, and I thought no one I knew would be there. (At the time, I was up for a very big job. I was in the running in a major way.) I had just come home from a weekend away and had left myself only a few minutes to get ready. I should have been dressed to the nines, but instead I barely looked like a 2. I was wearing a black-belted collar dress. It was fine. Not figure-flattering, not particularly stylish, and definitely not head-turning. It was really more of a day dress than something I should have worn to a dressy event. My hair was slicked back, and I was wearing very little makeup. When I'm not on TV, I don't normally wear a lot of makeup, but this gave new definition to the words "very little makeup."

I am sure you know what's coming. I ran into the executive producer of the show I was up for, an agent I was looking to sign with, and my ex-boyfriend's sister's husband (think about it; that's closer than you think). I was mad at myself the whole night. I have so many beautiful things in my closet and *that* was what I decided to wear?

I got rid of that dress the very next day—and everything else that wasn't a 10. Now if you open my closet, you'll see that every T-shirt fits me perfectly, every dress is as good as the next, and every pair of shoes is one I actually wear. I like getting dressed now. It is fun and easy. No matter what I choose, I know I'll look good.

Dana

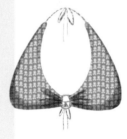

It's funny. I thought I lived my life by this step, but apparently I wasn't enforcing it enough. At this point, my closet was pretty much pared down, and I thought everything in it was a 10. Guess not. Here's what happened. One day when I was living in Miami, I was going out for a walk with my family. Miami is hot most of the time, but this was around Christmas, and it was a bit chilly. No heavy jacket needed, but I was wearing a tank top and jeans, and thought I might get cold, so I took along a swim cover-up in case I got cold. Mistake. While the beach cover-up was cute and sexy over a bikini, it was not so cute and sexy over my tank top and jeans. So, of course I got chilly, and even against my better judgment at the time, I donned the cover-up. I looked like I was wearing a big sack. Not a good look. You can guess what happened next. Yes, I ran into *him*. Miami is not only a beach town, but a small town, too. Oy! To make matters worse, he was with a friend from out of town. Not the best impression. Right then and there, I swore to myself that I would *never* again leave the house not looking and feeling my very best. And, yes, that cover-up is long gone.

- Is in keeping with your style
- Makes you feel confident
- Is in perfect condition
- Feels comfortable on your skin

Yes, it's a tall order, but once you've edited your closet to all 10s, dressing will be a cinch.

To make sure you never have a non-10 moment again, we need to get rid of all the items that are not 10s so that there is no chance you will grab one by accident,

10s

no chance you will grab one because you are being lazy, and no chance you will grab one because you just don't know any better.

You have no idea how good you are going to feel after you do this closet clean-out. You'll feel light: emotionally, mentally, and even physically. You are going to wonder why you didn't do this sooner. It's addictive, too.

round 1: condition

Let's get down to business. Before you even try anything on, do a once-over of every single item. You will be able to tell just by looking at some pieces that they go in the toss pile.

Does the item have stains or holes? Are your white T-shirts no longer white? Is the material worn or does it have pills (the nubs that form on sweaters)? Stretched beyond recognition? You can do away with those pieces. No question.

Toss the obvious. Does the item have stains or holes? Are your white T-shirts no longer white? Is the material worn or does it have pills (the nubs that form on sweaters)? Stretched beyond recognition? You can do away with those pieces. No question. There is no reason to wear anything for which you answered yes. You know you have better in your closet and that you deserve better.

round 2: style

Now that you've tossed the obvious culprits, it's time to delve deeper. In this round, you still don't try anything on. You and your sponsor are going to go through every piece in your closet (what's left after the first round) and determine whether or not:

- It is still even remotely in style.
- You think it represents your personality.
- You can see yourself wearing it again or at all.
- It fits your current lifestyle.

You could be the type of person who has a classic wardrobe—filled with things that pretty much never go out of style. The question is, are you or do you want to

be a classically dressed person? Also, will you actually wear those classic pieces? A classic suit may still be in style, but are you wearing a suit? Be honest.

On the other hand, you could be the type of person who buys every last trend. Your decisions about what to keep and what to get rid of may be more obvious. Trends come back, but never quite the same. (Remember the shoulder pads from the eighties?) Not to mention that when you wore the trend back in the day, you were probably ten or so years younger. At this point, your look may not be as extreme.

Back in step 3, you found your style. That will help you decide what to keep and what to toss.

Jill

I'll let Dana explain our first session doing rounds.

Dana

I have never laughed so hard. Jill and I started doing rounds in her closet when we were both living in Miami. Jill was getting ready to move to New York, and we were doing massive closet clean-outs. Closet space in New York City is woefully small, so we needed to unload everything she was not really going to wear. I mean there were suits, blazers, and sweaters that predated her move to Miami! Not only was most of it out of style and inappropriate for the climate she'd been living in, but when she started to try everything on and we saw how horribly it fit—all massive on her—we were rolling on the floor laughing so hard we were crying.

Looking back on all these clothes that you've collected, hoarded, and worn (or not) over the years is definitely cause for belly laughs. So don't be shy, and don't be embarrassed in front of your sponsor. His or her closet is probably just as bad. And if you think this is funny, just wait till you start trying stuff on!

round 3: fit

Now you are ready to start trying things on. This is going to take a while, so don't be surprised if you don't get through your whole closet in one session. This is why we booked your sponsor for a few dates in the calendar.

Start with either pants or tops. Leave on one pair of pants and keep changing the shirt, or wear a T-shirt or tank and keep trying on pants, jeans, and skirts. The process will go much faster this way, and you won't feel as exposed. This is about fit, not about putting together outfits. It's best to just put on a solid white T-shirt (if you have any left that aren't yellowed, torn, or otherwise worn out). Likewise, a pair of plain jeans or black pants will work when trying on all your tops.

Consider the feel of the fabric. If you couldn't tell by looking which pieces are itchy or uncomfortable, trying them on will remind you why you haven't worn them. Even if the piece was expensive or still fits, if it doesn't feel good against your skin, you are not going to wear it, or will wear it and be miserable. So dump it!

Move on to other areas. After you're through with pants and tops, try on dresses, bathing suits, cover-ups, pajamas, lounge wear, workout clothes, etc. Yes, pajamas. You are always a 10. Home alone or not! Don't forget jackets and coats. Wear what you would usually have on underneath—for example, a sweater. You need to see how everything truly fits before you decide whether to keep it.

Go through your bags, shoes, belts, and jewelry. You can and should try these on as well. The shoes that kill your feet, but cost a fortune? Try them on again, note how uncomfortable they are, or how out of style they actually are, or that they are some funky color that went with only one particular outfit that is now in the toss pile, thank goodness. Get rid of them. Seriously, there is no point wasting precious closet space on items you never wear.

Even though bags will never "not fit" you physically, they might not fit your current style. Maybe the bag went with a specific outfit that is now in the toss pile. Don't worry about how much these things cost when you bought them. If they are

Jill

I had a big problem getting rid of certain things. I had a lot of high-end designer blazers that I never wore. I tried on all of these expensive blazers (some were in good shape and still somewhat stylish, some weren't), but Dana kept saying, "When are you wearing these?" I do not wear blazers anymore for work. When I worked as a CBS sportscaster in Miami, I wore blazers. Now on the *Today* show, I wear dresses and pretty tops. Regardless, I found it hard to part with them. But I did. I consigned the blazers (ones still in style) and donated the rest to charity.

Dana

For some reason, when I bought all my nice coats, I bought them oversized. I think it was the style back when I bought them. The bummer is that they were gorgeous, classic, Calvin Klein wool coats (my sister was working there at the time, so I got a huge discount). I had a black-belted swing coat, a camel peacoat, and a black floor-length coat. I thought I'd have these coats forever. The reality is I had to get rid of them. Trying them on years later because I was living in New York again, I realized they didn't fit me. Fact is, they never had. Since I wasn't going to feel comfortable wearing them, instead of letting them sit there and clutter my closet, alas, I did get rid of them.

just sitting in your closet unused, they are worth nothing, at least to you (more on that later).

Maybe when you were younger you wore a ton of costume jewelry, but now you wear the real thing. Or since you've had kids, you don't wear much at all. Go through it all and decide what is "you" and what you actually wear. Often jewelry pieces have sentimental value because they were gifts (including to yourself) or were inherited. We're not saying to get rid of anything with special meaning, but if it's junky costume jewelry or you don't plan to ever wear it again, let it go.

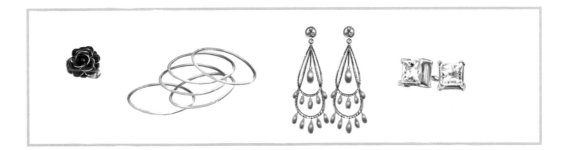

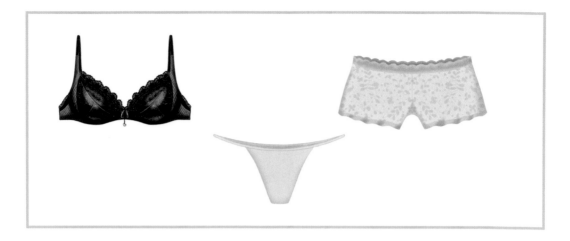

Underwear, slips, and other unmentionables. We won't make you do this with your sponsor if you're not comfortable, but don't forget to clean out this area of your wardrobe, too. The same rules apply. No holes, discoloration, bad fit, or bad style. What you wear under your clothes is just as important as what you're wearing on the outside. Undergarments set your mood and are the foundation of your outfit. Make sure they flatter you before you put anything over them. Bad underwear can ruin your whole outfit and your whole day.

Specialty items like your wedding dress. Keeping your bridesmaid dresses and graduation outfits? We know, we know. These are special to you, especially your wedding dress (though that's one you definitely will never wear again). Could you wear a bridesmaid dress again? Maybe. A graduation suit or dress? Possibly. Will you? That is the question. Think about it. These are not small trinkets. They are taking up precious real estate in your closet or storage space. We know you have pictures of these events in case you are ever feeling nostalgic.

If you're saving your wedding dress for your daughter, ask yourself whether you wore your own mother's dress. Need we say more? Look, a wedding dress falls

under exceptions, so we are not going to twist your arm. We just want you to be practical and realistic. Someone else might actually use your wedding dress—during this century—and you certainly don't need it.

We don't feel as forgiving about the bridesmaid dresses, graduation outfits, or any other specialty items that might be hogging space in your closet. We told you—honest and ruthless! Get rid of them.

not the last round

As you go through and try everything on, be as honest, objective, and ruthless as you can. And listen to your sponsor. You picked him or her for a reason. If the

Jill

I love costume jewelry. Love. You know who loves it even more? My mother. She has bags and bags (and bags) of sets of necklaces and earrings that match exactly. I love her. I hate "sets" of jewelry. I don't even know how she knows what she has. I have a ton of jewelry, but it is all well organized, each piece is a 10, and I wear all of it. I mentioned before that I love to wear all white, so accessories are my thing. They allow me to have fun with my outfits and show my personality. I like being the girl with the fun necklace. My accessories have been known to strike up conversations (not that I really have a problem with that!). Oh, and I'm trying to get my mom to mix it up a bit—to wear a bold necklace with studs, or big earrings with no necklace. A much better look!

Dana

I don't wear silver (or even white gold). I did when I was younger, so of course I used to have some in my jewelry box. I don't wear it anymore so I got rid of it. There is one piece, however, that I did keep. It's a sterling silver Gucci necklace that my Dad got for me in Italy when I was a child. Not only is it a gorgeous, very stylish piece, but it is extremely sentimental and special to me because it is from my father. I will never get rid of it.

sponsor says it doesn't flatter you, it probably doesn't. The reason you are trying on everything now, with a friend, is to get an invaluable second opinion.

After these first rounds, everything left in your closet should be a 10. There should be no question. The remaining pieces fit and flatter you. They make you feel like a million bucks.

Chances are, after you evaluate the condition, style, and fit of your clothes, you'll have a huge toss pile. That's OK. In fact, it's great.

It is so freeing to purge. This is your catharsis. Enjoy it.

But this won't be your last round through the closet. We know that wasn't what you were hoping, but it's the truth. This is your first and biggest clean-out, but it won't be your last. Once you do this big one, you can do little ones when necessary (maybe even by yourself once you know how). We like to do rounds at least twice a year. Spring and fall are perfect times to reassess.

There are other reasons to do rounds, too. People move, styles evolve, bodies change, clothes wear out or get dirty, and lifestyles change. Your closet is a work in progress.

Keep doing your rounds, so it will stay fun and easy to get dressed every day.

> After these first rounds, everything left in your closet should be a 10. There should be no question. The remaining pieces fit and flatter you. They make you feel like a million bucks.

STEP **6**

Giving Back

Are you still with us? *Good!* We're so glad. Truly, you've made it through the toughest part. We know it's been emotional, and we know it's been a lot of work, but hopefully you're starting to see the light at the end of the tunnel. That is, if you can see past the mounds of clothing in your keep and toss piles!

Jill

When I did my first round I had a huge maybe pile. But now I look at it like this: If I'm at all lukewarm about it, time to toss it (sort of like a guy!). "Maybe" just isn't good enough. I only wear 10s, not 9s or 8.5s, just 10s. Lukewarm includes pieces that are just not me. One time I bought this ridiculously sexy dress for an event I was attending with a certain movie star I was dating at the time (he will remain nameless). I felt I had to look like a knockout, so I went over the top with my outfit. I wore it that night, but knew I would never wear it again. It was really something, but I didn't feel comfortable in it, didn't feel like me, so I decided to let it go. Hopefully someone else is having a great time in it now! I probably had no business wearing that dress in the first place, but hey, I was twenty-eight and experimenting with my style.

Dana

I'm going to let you in on a little secret. In the process of doing my rounds I have gotten rid of some things that I have later thought better of. But I will also tell you that those thoughts were fleeting. For example, sometimes I'll remember a bag or a pair of shoes that I no longer own, and I'll wonder why I got rid of it. Not because I actually want to wear it, but because I just wonder why I don't have it. Silly, I know. (I used to have a collection of Anya Hindmarch bags. Seriously, I had at least six. Now I have one. I loved them, just hadn't used them in a while, so they ended up in the toss pile.) Then I just take a deep breath and let it go. That's it. The moment passes, and I have had a sweet thought about something that I once enjoyed and that now someone else is enjoying. I have other shoes and bags, the ones I actually use. End of story. Moving on.

Maybe

First get the toss pile out of sight to give yourself room to maneuver.

Do you still have a maybe pile? If so, go through all those pieces before we go any further. If you're even questioning a piece, throw it in the toss pile. Things you haven't worn in years should go. If you have second thoughts about an item's condition or whether it's still in style, dump it.

Now, what to do with that toss pile? We don't literally mean throw everything in the trash. Didn't your mother ever tell you that one woman's trash is another woman's treasure? Well, she may have been referring to men, but it holds true for clothing, too.

Just because these pieces no longer have a place in your wardrobe does not mean they are worthless. In fact, quite the opposite.

Let's make four piles: consignment shop, vintage shop, charity, and friends and family.

Go through the toss pile and sort it into destinations. We are going to walk you through it. Let's make four piles: consignment shop, vintage shop, charity, and friends and family.

consignment shops

If you buy top designer brands, you may have a gold mine in your closet. You probably have a ton of expensive pieces that were worn only once or twice, if at all (the tag-still-attached scenario).

How long you've had these items, and what they are, determines where you should take them. If they are a couple of years old, in good condition (not ripped, stained, or stretched out), and still in style, there's a good chance you can make back some of your money. These pieces were just sitting in your closet taking up space. They could be totally fabulous, trendy, designer pieces, but if you don't wear them, it doesn't matter. There could be a variety of reasons you don't wear them—you don't like the color or the print, they don't fit you well, they're too bold for your personality (or too conservative), or you thought you'd have more occasions to wear that kind of thing.

These clothes still have value. Get them to a consignment shop ASAP! Some consignment shops carry high-end merchandise, others carry mid-level, and others even less expensive items. Everything that you bring there must be *saleable*. That

Jill

Everything is in the presentation. I really believe that now. The first time I brought all my items to a consignment shop in the Hamptons, I brought too many things and a lot of the wrong things. I hadn't researched their merchandise, so I just took everything in. I had some really great pieces, but they were mixed in bags with a lot of junk. The store carries higher-end pieces, so my "good" items got lost because she had to weed through so much stuff that wasn't worthy of being consigned. I have learned, and now I go through my piles like I go through my closet, and carefully edit what I bring where. It saves time and makes it more likely that they will take my clothes.

Dana

I love to clean out my closets, but sometimes I find I have hung on to things longer than I should have. When I was living in Los Angeles, I used to try to resell my clothes at a store (actually a chain) called Cross-roads Trading Co. They go through your merchandise on the spot, and then, according to what they think it's worth, they give you your percentage in cash. That's the good news. The bad? They go through it in front of everyone else waiting on line. There have been times that the salesperson has gone through all of my clothes and not purchased one thing. Embarrassing. Oh well. There were plenty of times I walked out of there with a wallet full of cash. It's always worth trying.

means it must have value to someone, and the proprietor must feel confident about selling it. So before you bring anything anywhere, be honest about the condition of the pieces you want to sell. This will save everyone some time, and you some embarrassment.

Find out the level of merchandise the store carries: high-end, mid-level (recognizable brands but not highest level), and lower-end. Ask around or look online to research the consignment shops in your area. (Maybe you already shop at the ones near you.) Once you have your list together, make a few calls or better yet stop in to get a sense of the merchandise. This way, you will know which shop is best suited to carry your clothes and most likely to sell them. In person, you can get all of your questions answered so that when you bring in your items, the process will be quick and easy.

Usually consignment shops agree to take your pieces (the ones they approve) on loan. Some shops require you to make an appointment to bring in the clothes you want to sell. Others have a walk-in policy. The deal, usually, is that you get 50 percent of the sale price of whatever you have consigned, and the store keeps the other 50 percent. (Each shop has the right to decide the percentage, so ask the specifics.)

Make sure you are comfortable with the terms and the prices. But think about it like this: Isn't any money in your pocket better than clutter in your closet? Consigning clothes you don't wear is always a winning situation.

The sale price is agreed upon when you drop off your clothes, so you know what to expect when you get your check from the shop, when and if they sell your items. They don't charge their customers the original price you paid. They charge less, based on the proprietor's judgment of what the item is worth in the current market.

Usually the shops do their accounting once a month, and ask that you call on or after a specific date to find out the status of your merchandise. If pieces have sold, they will send you a check for your half.

They usually limit how long they will hold onto your merchandise. Each shop sets its own terms. If your pieces don't sell within the time frame (usually three to six months), you can pick up the unsold goods or they will donate them to charity.

Make sure you are comfortable with the terms and the prices. But think about it like this: Isn't any money in your pocket better than clutter in your closet? Consigning clothes you don't wear is always a winning situation.

vintage shops

Suppose you have designer merchandise—a Chanel bag, Hermes scarf, Gucci shoes—that's ten years old, or even twenty. Maybe it was your mother's or even your grandmother's. If it's in good condition, there is a market for it. Yes, really! These pieces are considered vintage.

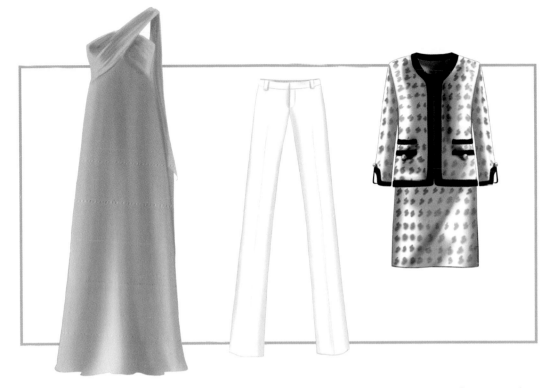

The items we just mentioned are all classic pieces, and on the surface sound like something you should keep. However, if the bag is in a color you don't like, the scarf is too conservative for your style, or the shoes are a size too small, you should not keep them. We don't care that they were expensive, or that they are high-end designer items. They are of no use to you and they are taking up precious closet space.

Vintage is more than accessories. You might have noticed that celebrities have been wearing vintage on the red carpet. Vintage designer gowns are in demand and super stylish. You might have a dress, a pair of amazing pants, or an old-school Chanel suit. What if it doesn't fit you well? What if the style was so your mother's taste, but not yours at all? Dump it.

But not in the garbage! You're going to try to sell these pieces, too. Vintage shops specialize in high-end designer, hard-to-find, and old-school pieces. There are some very well-known vintage shops in New York and Los Angeles. They are always written up in the magazines when celebrities talk about where they got (or borrowed!) their fabulous vintage gowns. In fact, there are popular vintage shops in many areas.

A vintage shop is a specialty consignment shop. It has similar policies on selling your merchandise and splitting the sale price. You could consign the pieces to a regular high-end consignment shop instead. However, vintage shops specialize in this genre of merchandise and have a reputation and a clientele that appreciates the value of these special pieces. So you'll probably get more for your pieces there.

Again, you may need to do a little bit of research to find a shop that suits your special pieces, but it will be worth it. Some very well-known vintage shops are Decades in Los Angeles, Resurrection in New York, and C. Madeleine's in Miami. There are great options all over the country, so search the Internet or ask your friends if they know any good options.

donating to charity

You may well have some current designer pieces in your wardrobe, and possibly one or two vintage items, but most of your toss pile won't have any real monetary value. Not that it isn't worth anything to anybody, but you are not likely to make any money from those pieces. That's OK. Really, it's a good thing. In fact, it's great! Here's where you get to give back.

Many people could really use your old clothes. They are not particular about the style or the size, or even necessarily the condition. They just need them. And you don't. So donate them to charity.

At tax time, you can deduct a percentage of the original value as a charitable donation. Ask your accountant what amount is appropriate. It's also important to get a receipt and to keep a list of the items and their original value. Charities don't put a value amount on the items, but you can.

Different charities take different types of clothes. Divide your toss pile into several categories. Even though all of these clothes are going to be dropped off and you will get nothing in return but a warm feeling in your heart and a tax receipt, you want them to find the right home. The key factor is condition.

Work clothes in good shape. These can be suits, but they don't have to be. Sweaters, skirts, and blouses in good condition that are office-appropriate can be donated to a charity like Dress for Success, which helps women who can't afford proper interview and work clothes get back on their feet and find jobs. These women are trying to make a good impression and get a job, so they need clothes

that are in perfect condition. The items don't have to be designer, but they obviously can't be ripped or stained.

Clothes in decent condition. These can be dressy or casual. Bring them to a thrift shop such as Goodwill or the Salvation Army. There are a ton of such charities in most areas. Try searching online to find your nearest options and call ahead. In many areas, they even pick up at your home! While you will not receive money from these donations, the charities sell them to raise money. While charities are not super picky about the items you bring, it would be nice to bring them clothes they can actually sell. Clothes in these stores are very inexpensive, so brands and trends don't matter.

Clothes that are functional and warm. These can be brought to home-less shelters and battered women's shelters. There are women out there who have literally nothing and can use anything you can donate. Do a little research online to find out where to bring the clothes in your area. Helping other women is alone worth the hassle of cleaning out your closets. Feel good that you have helped others and yourself in one fell swoop.

friends and family

You can also ask friends and family if they want to take a look at the toss pile. This group includes anyone you interact with who might be able to use the pieces you no longer need: your sister, mother, housekeeper, doorman, dog walker, babysitter, and

Jill

What do I do with the castaways that I don't donate or consign? My mother's friends take them. It is hysterical. My mom's friend Maureen camps out in my lobby waiting when she knows I'm doing a round. My Aunt Audrey, my mom's friend Edie, and my family friend Harriet all prance around in things I have given them. It is funny seeing them in items I, too, have stories about. They take pictures and tell stories about the places they've worn the clothes I give them. It's like the movie *Sisterhood of the Traveling Pants*. You never know where something might go!

Dana

When I lived in Miami, I used to give everything to my housekeeper. She would take all of it, and send a big box of all the clothes to her family in South America. You never know how far and wide your donations will reach and who or how many people you will end up helping.

girlfriends. Anyone you think might find a treasure in your trash. You never know. If they don't find something for themselves, they might be thrilled to find some new pieces for their family or friends.

You're not using it, so why not let someone else? We figure most people don't wear at least 60 percent of what's in their closets. What makes more sense: hoarding or donating? We hope at this point you agree that donating is the way to go. Letting go of your hoarding habit will make you happy and someone else happy too!

Making Fashion
Work for You

STEP 7

Getting Sane

Still OK? Just checking. Steps 5 and 6 can be a bit traumatic. It's tough to let go of old patterns, behaviors, and well, stuff. You did it though. We are so proud!

All that stuff you thought was your security blanket was really just dead weight bogging you down. You feel light and unencumbered. Now you're ready for a fresh start and a whole new look for your closet.

Time to get your closet organized and pretty. Then every morning when you open it, you won't say "ugh," but "ahhh."

> Time to get your closet organized and pretty. Then every morning when you open it, you won't say "ugh," but "ahhh."

get organized!

Now that you have pared your closet down to the keepers, you have some room in there. Don't worry, we are not saying that you can have only these clothes and can

never shop again! But first, organize the pieces you want to keep and will definitely wear and build smartly from there.

The first order of business is organizing your closet so that it is neat, efficient, manageable, and working for you.

Start by taking everything out. Yes, that's what we said. We're going to start fresh, as if you were moving into a new place. Yes, we know, this will be a bit labor intensive, but the work now will put you on easy street later.

Afterward, you'll feel so great! It'll be like the difference between looking into your oversize everyday bag and seeing a mess of cosmetics, receipts, jewelry, and loose change, and looking into your bag and seeing a cosmetics pouch, jewelry pouch, and wallet. In scenario two you can actually find your keys. Imagine that!

How do you feel when you get into your car and there is a half-empty coffee cup in the holder, half-empty water bottles rolling around on the floor, and random clothes, shoes, magazines, and what have you strewn on the back seat? Conversely, how do you feel right after you get your car washed, when all the coffee cups and water bottles have found their way to the trash, and you cleaned out the back seat so it could be vacuumed? A million times better, right?

When your life is cluttered, you feel disorganized, out of control, and constantly a step or two behind. In fact, clutter can be *why* you are late, frustrated, and generally a mess. When you are neat and organized, you feel totally in control and on top of your game. You are a well-oiled machine—on time, feeling

The first order of business is organizing your closet so that it is neat, efficient, manageable, and working for you.

Jill

I leave the house some days at five in the morning and don't get home until almost midnight. I need a lot of things to get me through the day, and I find it hard to keep everything organized. But I do. Here is my plan of attack. Every night, I take five minutes to figure out what I need for the next day. I take out those items and pack my bag. I don't need everything from my big makeup bag, just bronzer, lip gloss, and eyeliner. So I save some room by taking only my small makeup bag. Also, I do not carry around every gift card and airline frequent-flyer card I have. I leave those at home unless I'm planning a shopping day. Your wallet should not look like a stuffed cabbage. I carry with me only the essentials. I have a folder at home labeled "gift cards/certificates." Walking around with everything you own is not a good look. It is also totally inefficient. The five extra minutes of prep at night make my whole day better.

Dana

You can probably guess by now what I am going to say. Yes, my bags are always organized. I can't stand the clutter. Everything has its proper place, nothing is loosely floating around, and I *always* have my cell phone in the inside pocket. I know. Call me crazy, but you know what, I'm never in a panic over losing anything, never late, and always feel prepared. Oh, and two years into my lease people would still get in and ask if my car was new!

great, and ready to take on anything that comes your way.

If you felt this way about your wardrobe, just think what your life could be like! Let's get down to it.

We will assume your closet has at least one shelf and a hanging rack. We're hoping for more than that, but, yes, even if this is all your bare bones closet has, you can still be organized. On the other hand, if you have a fabulous closet, lucky you. If not, don't worry. We are going to get you organized anyway.

When your life is cluttered, you feel disorganized, out of control, and constantly a step or two behind. In fact, clutter can be why you are late, frustrated, and generally a mess. When you are neat and organized, you feel totally in control and on top of your game.

hang or fold?

The main reason to hang rather than fold is to keep clothes from getting wrinkled. Some pieces are actually better folded. The rule of thumb is to hang dresses, skirts, slacks, and blouses. However, certain materials, such as jersey (which many dresses are made of), should be folded. When jersey clothing is on hangers, it tends to grow. It stretches and becomes longer over time. If you really love your jersey dresses, fold them carefully and put them on a shelf. Before wearing a jersey dress, hang it in the bathroom with you while you take a shower. The steam and brief hang will eliminate the wrinkles.

Knit dresses should also be folded. You know what happens to your sweaters

if you hang them, right? You get those awful bumps at the shoulders, so the sweater looks like it's still on the hanger even when it's on your body. Not a good look! Fold them.

What to hang? The rest of your dresses, skirts (unless they are jersey or knit), blouses, slacks, and blazers. We don't want any of these to wrinkle, so hanging them is the best option. Now that you have all this hanging space, you will be able to see all of the individual items and give them the care and attention they deserve.

Here's what goes on the shelves: Everything else. No, just kidding. But seriously, fold and stack neatly your sweaters, sweatshirts, sweatpants, T-shirts, tank tops, long-sleeved T-shirts, workout pants and tops, and pajamas.

Jill

I have six cashmere sweaters—all perfect. I consider them an investment. I love the way they look, I love the way they feel, and I look forward to being cozy in them. Some are fitted, and some I wear as loungewear. I want to keep them all in 10 condition, so when I take the sweater off, it either goes to the dry cleaners or is folded neatly and put back in its place.

Dana

True story. I have two Missoni knit dresses. I travel back and forth to Miami all the time, and in the winter I usually leave a packed suitcase at my sister's. The clothes I need down there I certainly don't need in New York in the winter. (It also makes my niece very happy to see my luggage cause she knows that means I'll be back very soon.) In this bag I have bikinis, cover-ups, lightweight tops, a jean skirt, a pair of white jeans, yoga clothes, sandals, flip-flops, and a couple of dresses. Yes, I said dresses. Folded and packed nonetheless. I left one of my Missoni knit dresses packed in my suitcase all winter long. I wore it to our book party in December, and then again on Mother's Day in May. And you know what? It looked just as good in May as it did in December. You would never know it had been packed in my suitcase in the interim! Lesson: Don't be afraid to fold!

Items used once in a while or seasonally, like ski clothes, go on a top shelf (or under the bed). They'll be out of the way, they won't jam up your newly organized and beautiful closet, and when you need them you can break out the stepladder.

Some items can be either hung or folded, as you wish or have space for. Jeans, for example, will look the same whether you fold or hang them. Ditto for leggings. If you have enough room to hang them, it's nice to put them next to your slacks. That way, if you've decided that you want to wear pants, they are all in one place when you go to pick out an outfit. If you don't have enough hanging room for your jeans and leggings, they can easily be neatly folded and stacked on a shelf. Putting that pile on the shelf right above your slacks (if possible, and the closet is set up that way) will also give you an area devoted to pants.

by style and color

Now that you know what to fold and what to hang, we can make some logical and practical decisions about organizing your closet.

While you must hang all of your dresses together, it doesn't matter if they are all the way to the left of your closet or to the right. Put them where there won't be anything underneath, so they can hang free and clear without touching anything.

Group dresses by length first, and then by color. Hang the longest and dressiest dresses all the way to one side of your closet. You will probably wear these least often (it's not every day you are attending a black tie affair). From there, continue to hang your dresses according to length. Next will be your tea-length dresses, and then those that are just below and above the knee (which will likely be the ones

you wear the most often, now easier to see and reach). Within each length category, organize as best you can by color. You might have mostly black or you might have a wider variety of colors. Either way, group them in color blocks from dark to light or light to dark—all the black together, blue, on down to white. Easy so far, right?

Next to the shorter dresses, hang your blouses. If you're not wearing a dress, your next option is a top and either a skirt or pants. So logically your tops come next. Group first by style—long-sleeve, short-sleeve, and sleeveless, either in that order or reversed. You guessed it: Once sorted by style, they should be grouped next by color. Dark to light or light to dark.

Up next, your skirts. Again, group by length (this time short to long) and then by color. Why short to long this time? Well, we want to have your longest items closest to the outer edges of your closet so that in the middle (under the tops and short skirts) there is room below for shoes. You haven't forgotten about your beloved shoes, have you? Oh, and if you have built-in shoe racks or shelves, or some other fabulous setup for your shoes, excuse us—we are speaking here to the rest of us who are not as fortunate as you. But more on shoes later. Let's get back to the hanging rack.

Next up, slacks. Yup, dark to light. You're getting the hang of it! If you're hanging your jeans, it's your choice whether they come before or after the slacks. Either way, jeans together and slacks together. Group jeans by color wash—dark denim on down to your white jeans.

Right next to your pants, hang your blazers. We know, these are short, but chances are you have only a few of these and they are the last thing you put on, so mentally, it's nice to have these at the end.

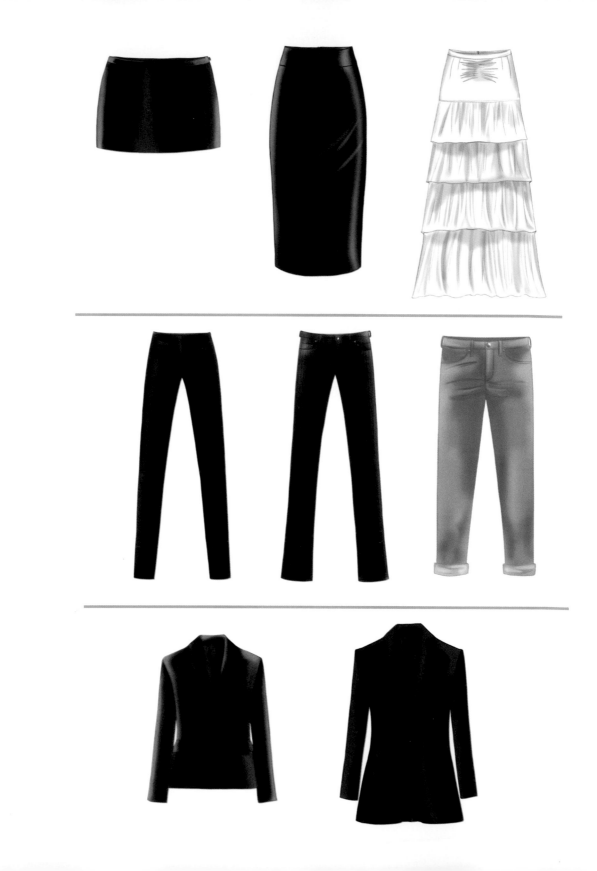

Now for the shelves. This part is going to be a little more open-ended because everyone has a different closet setup, but we will walk you through organizing your shelf/shelves according to a basic closet, which would have a shelf or two right above the hanging rack.

Group your sweaters together, then sweatshirts, sweatpants, T-shirts, tank tops, long-sleeve T-shirts, workout clothes, and pajamas. Let's not forget the jersey and knit dresses that should not be hung. Each category must be stacked according to color—darkest on the bottom, up to white on top (or vice versa). Before you put them on the shelf, make sure it's clean or lined!

The goal is neat, visible, and accessible. We want the system to make sense and make getting dressed stress-free. Above your hanging dresses, let's fold and stack your jersey and knit dresses. That way, when you are in the mood to wear a dress, even though they are not all hanging, they will be in the general vicinity and you will have a clear picture of all your choices.

Following that logic, let's fold and stack your sweaters above your blouses. That way, when you are looking for a top, all your options will be in full view.

The goal is neat, visible, and accessible. We want the system to make sense and make getting dressed stress-free.

Casual wear—your T-shirts, sweats, pajamas, and workout wear—can go above your pants. Just make sure these are all neatly grouped, folded, stacked, and organized by color. Why do even your sweats need to be organized by color? This is about more than just your sweats. It's about your peace of mind. The more organized you are in general, the better you will feel. It's a real thing! Trust us. You will

be thrilled by how different you will feel every day opening the door to an organized, sane closet instead of total chaos.

shoes, bags, jewelry, more

Just accessories and a few more bits to go.

Shoes. Let the fun begin! Organizing them is actually very easy. All your shoes should be stored in boxes. The boxes will then be organized by shoe style and stacked accordingly on the floor of the closet in the center under the blouses and short skirts. This way you can see and reach them all easily, and they won't be getting in the way of, and wrinkling, your longer dresses and pants. The boxes will protect them from getting dusty or smushed on the bottom of what used to be your shoe pile.

What? You no longer have the shoe boxes? Stores like Bed Bath & Beyond and The Container Store sell transparent plastic shoeboxes. We love these. Each pair of shoes gets its own box and, since you can see what's inside, it's easy to find what you're looking for. Stack each pile according to style—put your flats in one pile, your heels in another, boots in another. Depending on your shoe collection, you can go a step further by putting all of the closed-toe flat shoes together, then the open-toe flats, then the closed-toe heels, open-toe heels, and so on. To be totally efficient, take it to the next level and organize by color, dark to light or light to dark.

Bags are a bit trickier because the sizes range from large work totes to dainty clutches. If you have the shelf space, lining them up by size and color is the best plan. Start with the largest bags on the left, arranging them from dark to light or vice versa, on down to your smallest bags. If your clutches are getting lost in the shuffle or are too small or floppy to stand up straight so you can see them, you can always devote a drawer to them. Yes, a drawer! We'll get to that in a bit. If you don't have enough shelf space, you can store your bags in clear plastic boxes, ones larger than the shoe boxes.

Dana

I have always kept my shoe boxes. Before I transferred everything to the clear boxes, I used to take a Polaroid picture of each pair of shoes and tape it to the outside of its respective box so I would know which pair was in which box. This totally works, too!

Jill

If you think Dana is crazy, you are going to think I am totally nuts, but here it is. I have clear shoeboxes *and* I just bought a Polaroid camera to take pics of each pair of shoes and then tape the picture to the outside of each box. You might think I have too much time on my hands, but in the end this saves me time when I'm getting ready. Plus, I love looking at my closet and feeling totally organized.

You want your jewelry accessible and organized, yet not out as decor, ahem, clutter. Everyone's jewelry collection is unique, so we're going to give you free rein here to organize your pieces. That doesn't mean you can leave everything tangled together in one pouch or worse, in a plastic bag! No, no, no. Free rein doesn't mean your bracelets and earrings and necklaces can be strewn around your bedroom on the nightstand or dresser or hung from the mirror.

If you have space in a dresser drawer, get yourself some jewelry trays and lay everything out neatly, according to style—earrings in one tray, bracelets in another, rings in another, and necklaces in yet another, and so on for broaches or anything else you might have.

If you don't have drawer space, or a dresser for that matter, get yourself a hanging jewelry organizer. This is a gem! It has eighty see-through pouches, so you can give each of your precious pieces its own pouch. If eighty isn't enough, buy two. The best part is that they come on hangers, so you can hide them in your closet and they take up no room. When you are ready to accessorize your outfit, all of your jewelry will be completely visible and right there at your fingertips. No more being

Jill

I have a ton of closet space, so I store my purses in a hanging bag organizer that has separate cubby spaces for each bag. I am able to see each one easily, nothing is getting crushed, and I'm utilizing my space efficiently.

Dana

Mine are in the coat closet. Yes, I said coat closet. Which makes sense if you think about it. Your bag is the last thing you choose to polish off your outfit before you walk out the door. Truth be told, I have no other shelf for them! It totally works though.

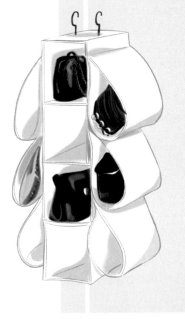

late or frustrated because you wasted fifteen minutes untangling your necklaces to get the one you really wanted to wear.

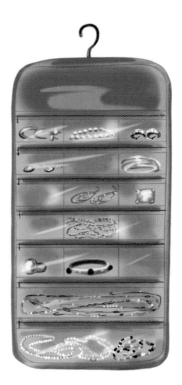

If you have a dresser, here's what goes inside: Underwear, bathing suits, socks, and scarves. Your clutches too, if you choose. Each category should have its own drawer. You can even roll your belts and put them in a drawer. If you prefer to have your belts near your pants, there are hanging contraptions for belts. It's up to you.

If you don't have a dresser, you can buy stackable drawers and put them in your closet. Problem solved!

All items in the drawers need to be organized as well. We are going to walk you through it.

Sort underwear by style and color. You can pile all the panties together according to color, and do the same with your bras. If you're the type who has matching sets, feel free to organize in sets. You can even separate underwear by occasion, such as everyday or special date. Just make sure that you can see it all so you can find the perfect undergarments for every outfit and situation.

Needless to say, but we will anyway, your bikinis should be placed in the drawer as sets and organized by color, your socks should be paired off, and your scarves neatly folded and organized by color.

Congrats, you made it! While we may have made you a little crazy on the path to sanity, this will all be worth it. We hope you can already see that, and we thank you for your patience.

STEP 8

Letting Go of
Old Ideals

Is everything in your closet a 10? Just checking that nothing slipped by when your sponsor wasn't looking!

OK, we're good. You've whipped your closet into shape. Soon when you open that closet door, the perfect outfit will just jump out at you.

You may be looking at all that new room and thinking, "My closet is empty! When do we get to go shopping?" Soon! First you need to learn a little more about fashion and a little more about *yourself*. That's so the next time you shop, you can shop smarter. You didn't do all that closet work for nothing.

dispelling old fashion myths

You've let go of your out-of-date clothes (thank you, sponsor!), and now it's time to let go of out-of-date fashion ideas. Getting dressed is very different than it was when your mom taught you how! The old rules no longer apply. Thank goodness!

For example, take the most famous rule: Don't wear white after Labor Day. Totally outdated. It is OK to wear white after Labor Day. In fact, it's downright chic.

> **It is OK to wear white after Labor Day. In fact, it's downright chic.**

White jeans paired with fall colors and materials—such as a beige chunky sweater and brown boots—are the perfect outfit for a crisp fall day. You can carry that outfit right through the winter.

The opposite is true, too. You can pair a cozy white sweater with a brown cords or slacks.

You've heard of winter white, which is actually off-white. A winter-white suit is often wool, so it's perfect for any occasion in the fall or winter. An elegant choice for the holidays, too.

However, white shoes aren't a good idea. Tough to keep clean, tough to balance an outfit that has a darker piece, and too much with all white. You're better off with a metallic shoe.

What about pantyhose? What about them? If you don't absolutely have to wear them (because of office dress code), or because you really don't like your bare legs, don't! That's right. Pantyhose are no longer necessary in this modern world. In fact, in this modern world we have something that can actually make you like your legs more. It's called self-tanner.

If you did some investigating, we're sure you'd find that even in the most conservative offices fewer women are wearing hose with their suits.

Jill

White is my best friend. I wear white *all* year-round. I think the concept of wearing white only between Memorial and Labor Day is silly and anti-quated. I wore a gorgeous off-white suit to the Emmys when I was presenting an award. (I was nominated twice, and then finally won!) The invitation read "black tie," and I knew everyone would be in a long gown or a cocktail dress. I looked completely different from everyone else, yet appropriate. When done right, white is the most chic, cleanest color you can wear.

Dana

I love white, too. My entire apartment in Miami was white. Most of my furniture is white. My bedroom is all white. Even my towels are white. So, you can probably guess that my wardrobe is, in large part, white. It could be from years spent living in warmer climates (Los Angeles and Miami), but I think it's just *me*. Most New Yorkers wear all black, but I decided when I moved back to the city that I was not going to succumb to the all-black uniform. I am happier wearing color and white. All winter I wear my white jeans, white cords, white sweaters, white puffy vest, and white scarf. That doesn't mean I never wear black. Don't get me wrong, black is very chic, very sexy, and can hide a host of sins, but even when going for a dark, more likely I will go for brown. It's more *me*.

Of course stockings can be sexy, and if you like this look, by all means incorporate that into your repertoire. Just know that you are free from the constraints of pantyhose in summer or any time of year. (They were never a good look with open-toe sandals anyway.)

You have a lot more freedom with fashion in general. Not only can you wear white whenever you want, and pantyhose never, but you can call your own shots most of the time. These days fashion is a lot less strict. Even rules on formal wear are looser.

Pantyhose are no longer necessary in this modern world. In fact, in this modern world we have something that can actually make you like your legs more. It's called self-tanner.

Now we have to find our own way. The road is less clear, but the good news is you can pave it yourself. On the other hand, when you get that invitation to a Saturday night wedding, it isn't as clear which dress to wear—a floor-length formal gown, a dress that hits just below the knee, or even a mini-dress. The answer can be any of the above!

When picking the perfect outfit, consider your lifestyle, body type, and personal style, but also consider the audience. Who is throwing the party, who is coming, where is it, when is it, what's the occasion? Back in the day, "black tie" meant a floor-length gown. Now the right choice is not so black and white. You must use your own best judgment. You can do it!

Here are some questions to evaluate the audience for an event. Is the host conservative or easygoing? Is the crowd older

or younger? Colleagues or close friends? Is the party on Saturday night, Sunday afternoon, or a weeknight? Is it at a fancy hotel in a big city or on a beach? Is it a wedding, a promotion, a birthday?

Take all this into account, plus what looks fabulous on you and expresses your personal style. Then you'll know whether you should wear the more traditional, conservative, floor-length gown or the younger, hipper, sexier mini-dress.

If you still can't figure it out, ask around. The host will always be happy to tell you what he or she is expecting. If you don't feel comfortable asking the host, ask anyone else who is attending. That way you will get a sense of the unofficial dress code.

> When picking the perfect outfit, consider your lifestyle, body type, and personal style, but also consider the audience.

why seasons are no longer relevant

We blew your mind with white after Labor Day and no pantyhose, but there's more! As your wardrobe is concerned, the seasons no longer matter in fashion.

You can now wear open-toe shoes all year long. Scandalous! Open-toe, high-heeled sandals are dressy and sexy, and you can and should, if you're comfortable, wear them whenever you get dressed up to go out at night. We're not advising you to run around all day in the freezing winter in open-toe sandals. If you are going to a holiday party, wedding, or dinner party, feel free to show off your pedicure!

So wear open-toe sandals in winter and boots in summer. You're getting the hang of it. Boots with skirts and dresses are all the rage —especially with light cotton dresses. Wearing boots with a dress smoothes the transition from winter to summer. Boots provide balance and warmth when it's not quite hot enough for a lightweight dress and sandals. Even in summer, boots are a great style choice and hip alternative.

You can now wear open-toe shoes all year long. Scandalous!

Have you seen photos of celebs wearing scarves around their necks even in the middle of the summer? This too has become widely acceptable and very fashionable. A scarf is a perfect accent piece, a great way to spice up your outfit and express your personal style. More than keeping you warm, scarves are a fashion statement. Worried you'll be too hot? Wrap it around more loosely and let it drape. You'll get all of the fashion and none of the faint. Again, this is a style choice, and it may not be your choice. We just want you to know you have options.

Having choices is *always* harder than not having them, but it makes fashion a lot more fun. You've always had a rebellious side. Rules were made to be broken, and now you can do just that.

In fact, you don't have to have two entirely separate wardrobes, one for summer and one for winter. Of course, some pieces are strictly for winter (a heavy wool sweater, a down ski parka) or summer (sundress, flip-flops), but most of your wardrobe works year-round. Shocking! How can this be? We have one word for you: layering.

Layering is dressing appropriately for the weather by adding or removing a layer or two of clothing. Just because it's mid-January doesn't mean you are relegated to wearing heavy, bulky, wool sweaters every single day. Try wearing a tank top under a cardigan or lighter sweater. As long as you have a warm coat, your

underneath layers can be lighter. The very same tank top that you wear under a sweater in winter you can wear on its own in the summer.

Dressing this way will maximize and modernize your wardrobe. You will get double duty from the same piece of clothing. This strategy takes less space in your closet, less money from your wallet, and less time transferring your closet from summer to winter and back again.

So wear that cardigan in the summer, too. It's the perfect layering piece over a lightweight dress for an air-conditioned office, or on a summer evening when it might cool off. Same sweater, double duty.

This seasonal flexibility gives you freedom to dress a little more creatively. There are endless combinations of colors and styles (and warmth) when you mix and match layers rather than just wearing a sweater.

Another great layering piece is a wrap. You can wear it around your neck as a scarf in winter or as a shawl in summer. In the spring and fall, throw it over a jean jacket for an added layer of warmth.

The no-season approach makes sense because it's often warm inside during cold weather and cold from the AC when it's hot out. You need both wardrobes all year, so you're better off finding clever ways to layer and adjust to keep comfortable.

Having choices is *always* harder than not having them, but it makes fashion a lot more fun. You've always had a rebellious side. Rules were made to be broken, and now you can do just that.

Jill

For the most part, I always feel hot, so being able to take off a layer allows me to be comfortable. Because I am mostly in dresses for work, I have devised a system. Most of my dresses can be worn all year-round. In the summer, I wear a dress, for example, a sleeveless, crewneck jumper, with nothing over it. If I am going straight from day to night, I tie a cardigan around my neck in case it gets chilly. In the fall and winter, I wear the same dress with a turtleneck, long-sleeve shirt, or white button-down underneath, a coat, and the same sweater tied around my shoulders but over my coat. I like the look (an alternative to the scarf), and I always have that sweater if I need it after I check my coat.

Dana

The thing I love about layering is being able to wear cotton in the winter! One of my biggest hesitations about moving back to New York was the winter. I had long since gotten rid of all my heavy sweaters, and the thought of buying new ones, let alone wearing them, was almost unbearable. I knew I needed to figure out another way to make it through the winter. And you know what? As long as I'm properly layered, I am warm enough, and I don't ever have to be itchy! Some of my sweaters and cardigans are blends (yes, I did buy a few), but I can wear cotton on the inside layer and can totally avoid wearing sweaters that are 100 percent wool. Also, I would rather wear a couple of layers and a scarf than wear a turtleneck. Heavy wool and turtlenecks make me feel claustrophobic and uncomfortable. If I'm going make fashion work for me, then not only do I have to look my best, I have to feel my best. If I'm not comfortable, I'm not happy, and that will affect my whole day.

rethink what looks good on you

Let go of what you think works for your body type, and learn what really flatters your figure!

Many people think they need to wear black or dark colors to camouflage their "problem areas." While it is true that black is slimming, it's not the only way to look thin.

The old school of thought was that if you are pear-shaped (carry more of your weight around the hips), you shouldn't wear white pants or jeans. Not true! You just need to know how. Try pairing the white bottom with a longer tunic top in a solid, darker color. The longer top will cover the area you are trying to minimize. You can also try wearing a flared-leg white jean that will draw the eye down the leg, away from the hip area.

Fashion designers (at least most of them) know that there are different body types out there. Fashion magazines may not show it (you may look through them and wonder who wears these clothes), but the stores have merchandise for everyone.

Take skinny jeans, which became all the rage several years ago. They're still popular, and if they look good on you, they're a definite fashion "yes." But notice that, even though they are trendy, they are not the only offerings in the jeans department. Not even close. Back in the day, the style was the style, and that was that. These days, *your* style is your style and you're sticking to it!

So if skinny jeans don't work for you, no worries. A plethora of jean styles is available nowadays. In order to be a 10, you have to be fashionable, not a fashion victim. If skinny jeans don't flatter you, or they make you uncomfortable, or they are just not your vibe, fine. In fact, great. Take a pass on that trend altogether. Don't buy them just to have them in your closet. They will just sit there. Every time you try them on you will just feel frustrated and uncomfortable. You won't end up wearing them. They will have been a total waste of money.

If you are apple-shaped (you carry more of your weight on your upper body), you might want to try a skinny jean. If you have great legs, show them off! By wearing a skinny jean, you are attracting attention to your lower half and away from the area you are trying to minimize. Skinny jeans paired with a black blazer that hits at your hips will provide balance and structure for your outfit and your figure. See how it works?

If you have a long waist (longer torso in proportion to your legs) there are ways to flatter your figure, too. Not only can you get skinny jeans, boot-cut jeans, and flared-bottom jeans, you can also get high-waisted jeans and pants. The high waist

will make your legs look longer and your waist area shorter, more in proportion. Pair the high-waisted jeans with a light-colored blouse tucked in to break up the long line of your waist, and you will look hot!

On the other hand, if you are short-waisted, try lower-riding jeans. They don't have to sit as low as the ones teens wear, just low enough to fit properly and comfortably. Nothing (namely your underwear) is going to accidentally peek out. For you, a low-waisted jean will elongate the torso and balance proportions. A longer top, untucked and hitting at your hip (rather than your waist) will further elongate your appearance, and will complement the low-waisted jean and your figure.

If you are petite, pick whatever jeans flatter you and pair them with a top in the same color. Pair dark denim with a navy or black top. Pair white jeans with a white top. This will make you look taller because the monochromatic scheme will create one long line.

If you're tall (we rarely hear complaints about this) and you'd like to break up your long, lean line, try wearing your jeans (any cut probably looks great) with a

top in a contrasting color. You can even tuck in the top and add a belt to further define the break from top to bottom. If you're wearing dark denim, pair it with a light-colored or white top, and if you're wearing white jeans, try them with a dark or black top. Any bold color will work with white in this case.

If you are plus size, there

are plenty of jean options for you, too. Follow the same strategies as above in your size.

So, you see, there is something out there for everyone. No longer are we limited by the dictates of fashion. Jeans are trendy in the sense that they are ubiquitous and generally accepted as the go-to staple, but there is no longer only one option.

The game has changed, and your mindset needs to change, too. Make the trends work for you. Don't feel trapped by what you think is trendy, because if you look a little closer, there really is something for everyone.

Don't be afraid to experiment. We just tossed all the old rules and myths out the window. Get current. Untuck your shirt, or lose the belt or shoulder pads. Wear flats—even at night or to a wedding. You'll find you actually want to dance!

Jill

As I mentioned earlier, my mother believes everything should match. She thinks your necklace should exactly match your earrings and bracelet, and your shoes should match your purse. She even loves outfits where the tops and bottoms are a matching set! (That's fine if you are five years old.) Although this makes life easier, as there aren't choices to make, the days of matchy-matchy are over. You will look stylish and put together when everything doesn't match *exactly!*

Dana

My grandmother is constantly reminiscing about "the old days" when people used to "dress up." Men wore jackets and ties, and women were decked out in heels and jewelry—and lots of makeup—just for dinner. It just isn't like that anymore, but she is still shocked every time we go out. I, of course, find this amusing and can't imagine having to be so formal every time I leave the house. I still want to look my best at all times, but I'm so thankful that pretty much anything goes these days as far as the dress code. You can be casual and still be a 10.

Discovering Your
Inner Fashionista

STEP 9

Shopping Smart

And now, the moment you've all been waiting for.

It's time to shop! But *slowly* and *smartly!*

You unloaded a lot during rounds, so there are probably some holes in your wardrobe. We want you to be prepared for any situation, occasion, or circumstance. Just because everything in your closet is a 10 does not mean that you have a fully functioning wardrobe yet. We are going to remedy that ASAP by adding pieces that will complement your personal style and prepare you for, well, your life.

what to add

You must be just as hardcore in your shopping decisions as you were in your closet clean-out decisions. Before you add *anything* to your beautifully organized and pared-down closet full of 10s, you must scrutinize it like you did every item during rounds. Ask yourself:

- Does it flatter my figure?
- Does it express my personality?
- Does my lifestyle warrant it?
- Is it comfortable?
- Is it age appropriate?
- Will I wear this color?
- Does it make me feel hot, sexy, elegant, sophisticated, stylish, and (insert adjective of your choice)?
- Does it represent my personal style?

If you can honestly answer "yes" to all of the above, then the purchase is probably smart.

Think quality, not quantity. Even though you're adding to your wardrobe, you don't want your closet to become an overwhelming mess again. You don't need a ton of clothes to always have something to wear. You just need the right clothes.

> You don't need a ton of clothes to always have something to wear. You just need the right clothes.

As you add new things, keep ditching old stuff. Your closet is a work in progress. It needs constant care and monitoring. Now that you know what works for you and what doesn't, this part of the program should be easy.

Old stuff goes out. New stuff comes in. The routine becomes second nature. You will know when it is time to let certain pieces go, and you will also know when and what to add.

ten basic must-haves

There are ten basics we think everyone must have in her closet. Choose them in your personal style.

Dark denim jeans. We covered styles of jeans in step 8, so you know there are styles to flatter every body type. If you have great legs and want to show them off, perhaps you like skinny jeans. If you are pear-shaped and want to draw attention away from the hip area, you want a boot-cut or flared-leg jean. Long-waisted? Try a high-waisted jean. And so on.

If you love and wear jeans, by all means have more than one pair, but for the basic must-have, we suggest dark denim. It can be dressed up or down, the dark wash is the most flattering color, and you can wear them all the time and no one will know it is the same pair.

Black blazer. Like jeans, this great basic is ubiquitous in the world of fashion. It can be worn time and again, is a great layering piece, and is always in style. Which is your style? If you have a great waist, try one that is fitted in the waistline.

If you are really tall, try a shorter one. If you are trying to elongate your midsection or make it appear slimmer, try a longer blazer. There is no one "it" blazer. The right one to buy is the one that flatters and expresses your best you.

LBD or little black dress. The LBD is going to be your new best friend. There is a little black dress for everyone! So let's find one that's perfect for you.

The beauty of the LBD is it can be strapless, sleeveless, short-sleeve, three-quarter sleeve, or long-sleeve. It can be one shoulder or halter. It can have a V-neck, round neck, plunging neck, or asymmetric neckline. The hemline can hit above, at, or below the knee. It can be any combination of the above. Options, options, options!

Again, choose one that flatters your figure. Want to show your legs? Go short. Want to accentuate your neck and chest area? Choose a V-neck. Don't love your arms? Choose one with a longer sleeve. There is a style for every body type. And black is flattering on everybody.

Bonus: These dresses can take you from day to night. You will be ready for

anything. Never again will you turn down an invititation because of your former mantra, "I have nothing to wear!"

Pair the LBD with your black blazer for the office. Last minute cocktail party? Check. Just remove the blazer, add some fun jewelry, and you're ready to party. Once you have this item in your arsenal, you will always be prepared. No more excuses. You will start saying "yes" more often, and will see how quickly your mood and your life change.

Black skirt. There are countless skirt styles, but for your go-to basic, choose a pencil skirt, A-line, or miniskirt.

If you want to show off your great legs, go for the miniskirt. If you want to camouflage your hip area, go for the A-line. If you want a sexy but office-appropriate classic, go for the pencil skirt.

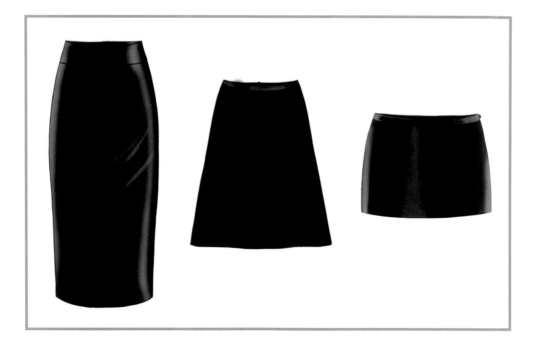

You can even pair your black skirt with your black blazer. Try a sexy camisole or pretty blouse underneath!

White button-down. We know what you're thinking. A white button-down is a white button-down. Not true. There are options even with these.

Fitted waist, straight waist, crisp, relaxed. The choice here is about body type, but even more about lifestyle. Where and how are you wearing it? Under a suit, tucked into jeans, tied at the waist over a bikini? Figure out which cut and material make the most sense for you.

Yes, you can pair this with your dark denim jeans, your black skirt, your black blazer. Put it under a sleeveless black dress! How about your white button-down shirt with your dark denim jeans *and* black blazer? Yet another piece of the wardrobe puzzle is in place.

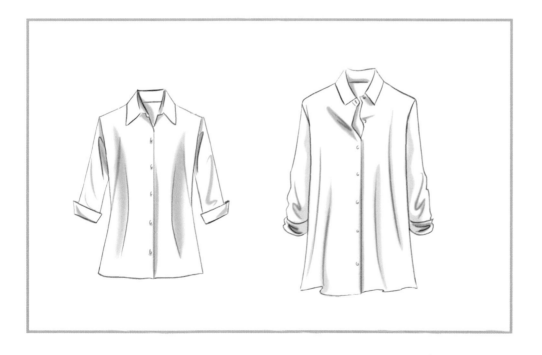

Black pumps. Black closed-toe pumps will work with anything day or night, casual or dressy. They will be the perfect complement to your dark denim, your black skirt, and even your LBD. Not to mention they will go with virtually anything in your closet.

Just because this is a basic black shoe does not mean it has to be boring. You can absolutely express your style and fashion savvy even with a basic pump. How high do you like the heel? Stiletto or kitten heel? Round toe or pointy? Any detailing?

Can you say "day to night"? Pumps work for the office and will take you anywhere you are invited afterward. LBD, black blazer, and black pumps by day; LBD, black pumps, and some fabulous jewelry by night. You're getting the hang of it!

Metallic strappy sandals. Again, a shoe that works with everything. Pair these sandals with dark denim jeans and a white button-down for dinner with friends (add the black blazer to the mix, or trade the jeans for the black skirt) or with a gown for a formal affair. Yes! The very same pair of sandals works for all occasions.

What works for you? High heels or lower? Silver or gold? Very strappy, or something a bit more secure? Your shoes, your style.

Black midsize purse. Buy one that not only represents your style but is functional. It will serve as an everyday bag, but should also move seamlessly from day to night. The right bag for you will hold all you need for the day, and take you straight to dinner or drinks without missing a beat.

Basic and neutral, this purse will be the one you reach for time and again, as it matches everything. You may use it every day. That's perfectly acceptable; in fact it's desirable. It's part of your uniform, so that's one less thing to think about.

Basic doesn't mean boring. Pick one that expresses your style. Do you prefer structured or more of a hobo style? There are countless varieties. The right purse will work with all of your other basics because they are all you.

Metallic clutch. Perfect for evening or a formal event, a clutch can also be used during the day if you are traveling light (translation: no work and no kids).

Choose gold or silver. Your best bet is to pick the same metallic as your strappy sandals. This way you will always be appropriately accessorized and true to your color palette. Since metallics are neutrals, you will have no problem incorporating them into your wardrobe.

Pair the clutch with the LBD and strappy sandals or with the black blazer, white button-down, jeans, and pumps. Try different combinations to see what works for you.

Jill

I have an LBD I bought a decade ago. Not exaggerating, it was ten years ago. I was twenty-four, living in Miami, and I was going to some big party. It was on the sale rack. Original price $750, marked down to $250, then an additional 20 percent off. I hit the jackpot! It fit me perfectly and it was so fabulous. This year I threw a big birthday party at my home. Guess what I wore? Yes! The LBD. I thought about looking for something new and ultra-fabulous, but I decided on the LBD. It is still intact, still fits perfectly, and is still a 10!

Dana

I am still wearing the same gold metallic sandals I bought for my sister's wedding twelve years ago! Yes, it's true. They are the most comfortable heels I own, and they match *everything*. I have nicknamed them my "wedding shoes" because I always wear them to weddings—in addition to a million other places. This is where quality, not quantity, really comes into play. They are beautiful Michel Perry sandals. They have a ring that goes around the big toe, which gives them a bohemian vibe. They couldn't be more me. Luckily, I got them on sale at the Barneys warehouse sale. But even if I hadn't, they would have been worth it. I have certainly gotten my money's worth and then some. I always think investing in expensive shoes is smart. They really are of superior construction, so will stand the test of time, and (if you buy the right size) way more comfortable.

Don't be afraid to pair your metallic clutch with your black pumps and your black purse with your metallic sandals. Remember the days are over when your shoes and bag have to be an exact match. It doesn't mean they can't match, it just means they don't have to, so express yourself.

Wrap. These days it's often called a pashmina, after one of the materials wraps are often made of. The wrap can also be used as a shawl, scarf, or sarong. It is a great layering piece. It can be worn over your LBD, over your white button-down, or even over your white button-down and black blazer. It can be wrapped around your neck as a scarf or even used on the plane as a blanket. It is most versa-

tile, practical, and handy, not to mention quite stylish.

We suggest a neutral color like black, ivory, or grey. This is another item you will wear all the time. It can be easily incorporated into your wardrobe and will never go out of style.

These ten must-have basics are the building blocks of your wardrobe. You can mix and match them with each other and anything and everything else in your closet. Because they are solid and neutral, you can wear them over and over without anyone noticing. The best part is that they provide you with a blank palette on which to accessorize and express yourself.

We know that your wardrobe will encompass more than just these ten basics, and that your style will reach further than these staples will take you. Just understand that each piece can create a different look depending on what you pair it with, and know that no matter what, your closet will never hold you back again.

Once you have these pieces in your rotation, you will always have the ability to choose an outfit. You will always have an appropriate option. And you will know how to strut your style. Just think of the opportunities!

spend on classics, save on trends

Invest wisely in the ten must-have pieces. They will be the backbone of your wardrobe. You will have them for a long time and will wear them often.

They must be high *quality*. You don't want them to wear out, stretch out, or in any way look anything less than a 10. Of course they will not be the only pieces in your wardrobe, but they will get the most play, so you will count on them to make you look good and feel good.

We cannot stress enough that it is worth it to spend a little bit more on these pieces. That doesn't mean you have to go beyond your clothing budget. But you get what you pay for. For the must-have pieces, it is worth paying a little more.

The same is true for other basic pieces in your style category. Classic pieces can be anything from jeans to a trench coat.

If you can get the right items on sale, great! Sometimes even the classic basics go on sale.

However, a sale price is not, repeat *not*, a reason to buy something. That's where we got into trouble before. Don't kid yourself. Just because you are getting a great deal doesn't mean you are going to wear it.

Stores are always receiving new merchandise and need to make room, so sometimes you can find exactly what you need on the sale rack.

However, a sale price is not, repeat *not*, a reason to buy something. That's where we got into trouble before. Don't kid yourself. Just because you are getting a great deal doesn't mean you are going to wear it. We recall a closet filled with clothes with the tags still on them, and

Jill

I do not love my legs. You will rarely see me in a short skirt (and never in shorts, yikes!). However, when I was doing a story on outlet shopping, I stumbled upon this adorable miniskirt. And yes, it shows my legs. But I loved it and I said to myself, "It really doesn't belong in my closet, but it is so cute and I can wear it with a fitted T-shirt." I bought it (half-price). I will wear it and have fun with it even though it is not something I would normally wear. The point of the story? If you are going to purchase something so out of your comfort zone you better really love it and love it on *you!*

Dana

I know, I know, practice what you preach. And for the most part I do! We're all a work in progress though, right? As I mentioned earlier, for whatever reason I don't wear belts, silver, T-shirts, or anything red. Just don't. So you would think I wouldn't buy these items. Well, I don't. Except for this one time recently. I got caught up in one of my favorite stores, Calypso, and there were some things on sale. I know! But, anyway, there was this really sweet belt. It was white with two gold shells as the buckle. Well, I don't wear belts, but I do wear white, and I do wear gold, and I do love shells. (Anyone who knows me knows that anything beachy is my personal theme.) So the three things I loved outweighed the one I didn't, and I bought the belt. Did I mention it was on sale? It was the kind of scenario where I got caught up in the moment, and swore up and down to myself that I would find a way to wear it. The salesgirls in there all know me, and they were equally convincing. Truth be told, I have not yet worn the belt, and it wasn't even marked down that much. Oh well. I'm not getting rid of it. I will find a way to wear it, eventually.

lots of clothes that weren't exactly your color and didn't fit exactly right. Wonder how those got there?

Go forward, not back there! Follow the checklist at the beginning of this step

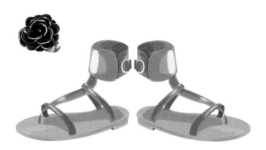

to evaluate the item. The same rules apply to sale merchandise.

Spend a little more on quality must-haves and any other classic basics that will serve you equally well and long, and spend a little less on the trendier items. Don't spend as much on the fun piece of costume jewelry or the "in" summer sandal.

In fact, spend a lot less. You'll probably wear trendy items for a season and then chuck them. That's what makes them so much fun. You feel and look current, on trend, and in step with everyone else. But since trends are fleeting, to invest heavily in these pieces is totally unnecessary.

Just like the classics, trendy items (inexpensive though they may be) must be a 10. If they don't fit, flatter, and otherwise make you look and feel great, they don't make the cut.

While the high-end designers are producing the trendy pieces, so are the mass-market chains. Why spend a ton on something that you don't need to last more than one season? Indulge in the trend, but don't indulge your wallet.

Like the sale items, buy the cheap and trendy items only if you are actually going to wear them. Cheap, trendy, and *you* is OK. Not you? Not OK. You have room in your closet now, but that is no excuse to go on a massive shopping spree and fill it with junk!

Just like the classics, trendy items (inexpensive though they may be) must be a 10. If they don't fit, flatter, and otherwise make you look and feel great, they don't make the cut.

your uniform

Your "uniform" is your go-to, everyday look. You build it by combining basics with other pieces that reflect your personal style. This is true whether you are a classic girl, bohemian, preppy, fashionista, surfer chick, or soccer mom.

Let's take dark denim jeans, a basic must-have that's probably the most widely worn item of clothing. Regardless of your style, you will probably have a pair of jeans in your uniform. What you pair with it will show your own personal style.

If you're a classic girl, you might pair your jeans with a white button-down shirt. This would be your uniform. Your go-to outfit, your everyday look, your comfort zone. Accordingly, you will invest in more than one white button-down. You might even buy a black one or a tan one too, but you will concentrate your wardrobe around these pieces.

The bohemian girl will pair her jeans with flowing peasant tops. She will likely have many. Some will be sleeveless, some short-sleeved, and some long. They

will mostly be white, but she will have some color options too, whichever colors are in her particular palette. This is her look, her vibe, her uniform.

The preppy girl is most comfortable in polo shirts and cable knit sweaters. Again, this is her uniform. She will pair them with jeans too, but her look will be entirely different. She will have shirts and sweaters in an assortment of bright and pastel colors, as that is her comfort range and expresses her style.

The fashionista pairs dark denim with a variety of chic black blouses. She might have many, and they might all be different, but the look will be the same. The uniform and style will be clear.

The surfer chick is probably the most casual. If she is actually in jeans (and not in a bikini) she will pair them with a variety of tank tops and tube tops. The tops probably have vintage logos and designs reminiscent of seventies California and Hawaii.

The soccer mom's top of choice will probably be some form of a T-shirt: short-sleeve, long-sleeve, three-quarter sleeve, or even V-neck. T-shirts are comfortable and work perfectly with the lifestyle. She prefers solids and darker colors, and might spice it up with some stripes or fun colors every once in a while.

See how it works? Accessories, shoes, and jewelry will also express your style. Once all of these pieces are in place, and your go-to outfit becomes like a uniform, you will not believe how easy it is to get dressed every day. No matter where you are going, or what you are doing, you will always look like you.

Of course, you do not have to wear the same thing every day. But your go-to outfit is your go-to outfit for a reason. It makes you feel most comfortable and most like *you*. It is the look you gravitate toward while the other clothes end up sitting there—taking up space, having wasted your money.

When you dress in a style that best expresses "you," you become your best "you." You are most comfortable, expressive, confident, and sexy. You become a living, breathing, walking 10. What's better than that?

The whole point of steps 1 to 8 was to get you here, ready to find the look that best expresses you.

When you dress in a style that best expresses "you," you become your best "you." You are most comfortable, expressive, confident, and sexy. You become a living, breathing, walking 10. What's better than that?

undergarments you need

One more area we need to cover (literally and figuratively) is undergarments. While you'll have personal preferences here, you do need the right foundation. Bad underwear can ruin your whole look.

If you are wearing anything white, sheer, or tight, wear a seamless nude (or skin-tone) bra and panties. Every woman should have a supply. They blend in for an even, solid look and don't reveal anything you don't want to.

If you are wearing a tight dress, sheer skirt, or white shirt and white jeans, you may need a bra and panties or thong, a full slip, or half slip. The coverage is up to

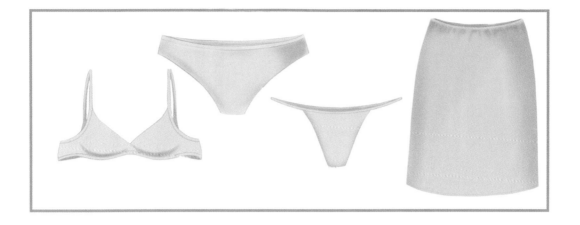

you. We just want you to be a 10: comfortable, appropriate, classy, sexy, confident. Don't discount how important a role your undergarments play in this.

Strapless dress? Strapless bra. It's that easy. Whatever your outfit needs, there is an undergarment solution out there.

If you want added support, try body slimmers. These come in all shapes and sizes and there is one for any need. Whether you want to tighten your belly, thighs, arms, or bust, there is a body shaper for you. It's a very worthy investment.

What we don't want: panty lines, exposed bra straps, muffin top.

That's the bare minimum for your under-wear drawer. The rest is up to you. If you tend to wear darker colors or thicker tops, feel free to experiment with black, color, or even lace.

Whatever makes you feel special will add to that confidence we are talking about. Even if no one else sees what you have on underneath, you will know, and that's the most important thing.

Don't think that if you're single, or married even, it doesn't matter. It does. Fashion is a mental game as much as it is about anything you're wearing, so get in the game.

To go a step further, if you don't normally do it, try wearing bra and panty sets, and see how that makes you feel. Sexy? We thought so. Dress up for yourself and see how much better you feel. Trust us. It makes a huge difference.

We know that figuring out your style and rounding out your wardrobe with the appropriate pieces and undergarments can be overwhelming. Take a deep breath. You don't have to buy everything in one shopping excursion. In fact, don't! Filling in your wardrobe is going to take time. Your wardrobe will always be a work in progress. Just like you didn't unload everything from your closet in one day, or even one week, we don't expect or want you to fill it back up all at once. Take your time and buy the right pieces. You will know them when you see them. Don't be in such a hurry. Remember, quality, not quantity.

Working It

At this point, you have your everyday uniform down, easy as pie. Now let's get ready for the out-of-the-ordinary occasions. In steps 10 through 12 you will learn to dress for work, fun, and romance.

We will help you make a plan that's right for your style. We also highly recommend trying on the options in front of a sponsor or friend. Whenever you need or want to look extra special for an occasion, enlist the help of your sponsor or anyone else you trust. Have this person come over, try on every outfit you are considering wearing, and together pick the winner. This will alleviate any anxiety you might be feeling and boost your confidence. It's good to have a second opinion. When life is crazy, exciting, or overwhelming, it helps to have reinforcement.

In this step, we are going to deal with all manner of special situations related to work. Whether it's an interview for the job of your dreams, the first

Whenever you need or want to look extra special for an occasion, enlist the help of your sponsor or anyone else you trust. Have this person come over, try on every outfit you are considering wearing, and together pick the winner.

day at a new job, the annual company picnic, or the office holiday party, we are going to get you there in style.

job interview

First things first. Back in the day, you were probably told that you needed an interview suit. Well, remember back in step 8 when we tossed outdated fashion ideas out the window? This one went there with the rest of them. There is no longer one right outfit to wear on an interview.

We know it can be tricky figuring out what to wear to an interview. Office attire in general has changed with the times. It is less conservative and formal. This is actually a good thing! Just think, the office is another opportunity for you to express yourself and be comfortable in what you're wearing, rather than feeling like you are in some sort of costume, trying to make a certain impression.

Don't get us wrong, you are always trying to make an impression, especially in a job interview, but at least this impression will be of you, the *real* you, the best you, not a cookie cutout of what an interviewee should look like.

Going on a job interview is nerve-wracking enough without throwing outfit worry into the mix. Let's take the fashion confusion out of the equation so you can focus on your talking points and questions and showing them your overall brilliance.

The key: When you prepare for a job interview, take into account not only your style and personality, but the field. This is a prime time to know your audience. As we said, you are trying to make an impression. Who's your interview with, and what will he or she consider appropriate dress? Consider the fashion environment in that particular office, and that industry in general. If you are currently working in the field, you probably understand the appropriate level of dress. If you are just starting (or getting back into) your career, you might have to do a little research to figure out what's appropriate.

Just think, the office is another opportunity for you to express yourself and be comfortable in what you're wearing, rather than feeling like you are in some sort of costume, trying to make a certain impression.

There are three levels of office style: edgy, corporate, and casual. Edgy style is for entertainment, music, and the like. In creative fields, the style environment tends to be creative too. Expressing your personality through your wardrobe is right for the gig. Corporate is appropriate for lawyers or bankers or a conservative profession. Casual is for teachers, freelancers, yoga teachers, you get it.

Dana

I have to admit I bought two suits my senior year in college. My grandmother insisted that I have them. They were so not me, but what did I know? Of course there was the requisite ivory blouse. I don't remember exactly how this came about, but my ivory blouse became the "lucky interview blouse." Again, it was *so* not me, but I wore the blouse to my interview at *Mademoiselle* magazine, and I got the job! I kept the blouse, and when my sister was going on an interview for a job at Calvin Klein, she wore the lucky blouse, too. And she got the job! By the way, the blouse was not especially fashionable, special, or different, but I guess it was lucky. We have since parted ways with the blouse, but whenever either of us has an important meeting or interview, we always joke that we should have saved it.

Jill

I agree with Dana. The days of the interview suit are *over*. I don't know exactly when I went from being the interviewee to the interviewer, but I am now meeting with girls who want to break into the fashion world and graduates who are looking to get into broadcasting, marketing, or public relations. Friends of the family constantly call me saying, "So-and-so is going in to meet with X about a job. Does she have to wear a black suit?" The answer is no. I am not saying to wear your sexiest dress, but wear something in the middle that will express your personality. I cannot think of one scenario where a button-down shirt with a pencil skirt and pumps wouldn't be acceptable. To me, it looks generic to just wear the obvious interview uniform. Be creative when it comes to certain events and occasions. The worst thing you can be is forgettable and predictable. Clothing is one thing you can actually control in any situation!

The key: When you prepare for a job interview, take into account not only your style and personality, but the field. This is a prime time to know your audience.

Let's put together a basic interview outfit that will work in most scenarios, except ultra-corporate or ultra-casual. This covers most bases, and so will this outfit. Guess what? If you've been following directions, you already own everything you need.

Let's head into your closet. Your ten basic must-haves will provide four or five pieces for your interview outfit. Fill in with personal style pieces from your uniform. It's simple, and this outfit should be, too. Chic, stylish, but simple.

Pair your black blazer with your dark denim jeans or black skirt. It depends on how dressy the company is, which you'll find out in your research. Jeans versus skirt is also a personal preference. You might feel more like a power player in a

skirt, or more like yourself in your dark denim.

Add your black pumps and your black mid-size everyday bag. (That's four basics.)

Go for a traditional pump if you are a classic girl, or the latest stiletto if you are a full-on fashionista. Whichever you choose, make sure you are comfortable, feel like yourself, and, most important, can walk! You want to feel and look confident and in control as you breeze in and out of the room. No wobblers need apply.

For the bag, whatever your style, make sure it is organized, cleaned out, and big enough to carry your files, resume, and whatever else you will need. You want to have easy access to papers or materials you might need to produce during the course of your interview. You also don't want to look like you're schlepping everything you own. Your bag should be big enough to carry what you need, but not look like an overnight bag. For an interview, you might choose something with a bit more structure than usual, though the general design and detailing are up to you. You know your style. You know you're a 10. Go with it. Express yourself. And get that job. You deserve it!

The only decisions left are your top and jewelry. That's where your style uniform comes in.

If you are a classic girl, you will probably wear your white button-down shirt under your blazer. You may add your thin leather belt, diamond studs, and leather strap watch. Keep it classic and keep it you.

Bohemian girls, you may choose to wear a top that is a little less structured and a little more feminine. Perhaps a white sleeveless peasant top or pretty camisole. Add your gold bangles and layered gold chain necklaces, and you will be sure to show your style.

Preppies, you might wear a lightweight pastel crewneck sweater under your blazer. Add your pearl necklace and you will certainly look the part.

Fashionistas, we know what's going underneath your black blazer. More black! You will likely choose a chic black top and a fabulous statement necklace, earrings, or a cocktail ring. Pick whatever jewelry works best, but choose only one piece. Remember, chic and simple. You want them to see you, not your jewelry.

Surfer chicks, you might choose a pretty tank top with your blazer. Keep it solid and in a muted tone. You are at a job interview, not the beach.

Soccer moms, a white, fitted T-shirt will show your clean and easy style. Some small earrings will complete the look.

Let's say you are going to interview at a law firm or a big corporation. We already know that you are going to wear a suit. Your suit doesn't need to be stuffy, but it does need to show them you mean business. Show them your confidence and style. No matter what your individual style is, this suit should have a current cut, fit you perfectly, be tasteful, and be a solid, neutral color. You should feel comfortable (as if you could wear it to work every day) and successful (as if you already have the job).

In any fashion environment, you can choose a pantsuit or a skirt suit.

CLASSIC GIRL

BOHEMIAN GIRL

PREPPY GIRL

FASHIONISTA

SURFER CHICK

SOCCER MOM

What you wear underneath is also up to you. Express who you are within the parameters of the culture of the workplace.

If you are interviewing in a field where the look is casual, you want to look the part just the same. If you will be standing on your feet all day in front of a classroom or in a retail store, no heels! For a job interview in a casual environment, you can take it down a notch and lose the blazer.

The exception (for interviews in all work environments): flip-flops. These are everywhere from the beach to the city. We all love flip-flops. They're cute, comfortable, and fun, but please no flip-flops on a job interview. Even you, surfer chicks! It may be OK to wear them once you have the job, but they are really inappropriate for an interview. Thank you.

It is better to be overdressed than underdressed, especially for a job interview. You'll have plenty of time to express yourself once you get the job.

Are you starting to get the hang of it? All of the above outfits are based on the ten basic must-haves and the pieces you should be adding according to your uniform. Extra suits may be needed in certain industries, but otherwise your work clothes can overlap with your must-haves and everyday uniform. All of these pieces should be in your wardrobe, and they should all be 10s.

first day at a new job

Got the job? Good for you! We knew you would. Now what to wear on your first day? You still want to make an impression, so let's make that outfit count. Remember how important your outfit was on the first day back to school? It's kind of like that, only for grown-ups.

Whatever you wore to your interview can guide what you wear the first day on the job. You were dressed up (maybe more than on a normal day) and want to show up that first day looking much the same. There should be no mistake about who was hired for the job. Your boss wants to see the person he or she met in the interview. (Translation: If you wore a suit to the interview, wear a suit on your first day. If you had to wear a suit to the interview, likely you will be wearing one every day you are at that job. Not your vibe? Maybe it's not the career for you. But that's another story altogether.) You will also be meeting the rest of the staff that day, so you want to make the best impression. (Remember, it's always better to be a little overdressed than under.)

If you dressed it up for the interview, but are going to be finger painting with toddlers on your first day, by all means dress it down. This doesn't mean come to work in the clothes that should have been in the toss pile. Just come prepared for what you will actually be dealing with that day. Sitting behind a desk wearing a red top instead of gray is fine. Coming to work in a stained sweatsuit, not fine.

That said, if you want to jazz it up a bit and show a little more of your personality, go for it! Want to wear a color instead of a neutral? By all means do. Want to wear a funkier piece of jewelry or a less conservative bag? Be our guest.

We hope that when you were at the interview you got an even clearer picture of the office fashion vibe, so if you feel safe experimenting with something a bit bolder and more *you*, go for it.

If you feel well versed in your new office's fashion vibe and you want to change it up entirely from what you wore to the interview, that's fine too. Here are some ideas.

If you are a classic girl, you want to show that off, so maybe you will choose a sexy fitted pencil skirt and white button-down, with your fabulous black pumps and black bag. Your jewelry doesn't really change, so you will stick with your diamond studs and leather watch. Perhaps you will express yourself with a printed silk scarf around your neck or even tied to your purse.

Bohemian? Try a pretty, romantic dress and gold sandals or boots. Pair them with some gold bangles and long, layered gold chain necklaces and a less structured (but neat and organized) hobo bag.

180

Jill

E ven though I don't work in a corporate environment, I still need to look the part. A certain level
of dress is expected of me. Most often you will find me
in a dress at work. Dresses have become my work
uniforms. I change them up with a piece of statement
jewelry, grab my heels out of my bag just when I need
them, and I'm ready to go.

Dana

I could never in a million years wear a suit to work every day. It's just not me. Luckily I picked a career in fashion and entertainment, where I can dress in a way that is both fun and comfortable. I'm almost always in flats and either jeans and a flowing top or a dress depending on my mood, the weather, and whether or not I'm on a shoot. How you feel everyday when you go to work is hugely important. I love that I can wear my uniform every day, feel totally put together, feel totally confident, and feel completely like me.

CLASSIC GIRL

BOHEMIAN GIRL

PREPPY GIRL

FASHIONISTA

SURFER CHICK

SOCCER MOM

Preppy girls might want to wear white jeans with a cable knit sweater. Some Jack Rogers sandals or ballet flats, pearl studs or a pearl necklace, and a tote will complement your look.

The fashionista will go for all black. She might choose a stylish black dress, or she may go the chic, trendy black pants and blouse route. She will definitely break out the stilettos (pumps or sandals), and her black bag will be the one in all the magazines. As usual, she will accent with a great statement necklace, a pair of fabulous earrings, or maybe a chunky cocktail ring.

If you're a surfer chick, you still want to be work appropriate, but if you can get away with it you are going to show them who you are. You might pick a jean skirt with a pretty tank top and flat sandals or boots. You might wear a chunky silver ring or cuff bracelet and carry a less structured purse.

The soccer mom might want to keep it simple and go for a shirtdress or wrap dress. Easy, breezy, and low maintenance. She will pair it with simple, midsize heels, either black pumps or her metallic open-toe sandals. She will also have a structured and organized midsize everyday bag. (No oversized, unnecessary diaper bags!) Her jewelry will be simple.

These looks are all subject to the fashion climate of whatever particular office you are going to work in. We can't stress enough how important it is to know your audience. You may need to dress it up or even down a bit.

company picnic or summer outing

No matter what your occupation or what your style, for the company picnic or summer outing you want to look like you came to play. You want to come across as a team player in more ways than one.

Whether you work for Wall Street, a record label, or a public school system, a picnic is a picnic. Of course there will be socializing and food, but chances are good that there will also be sporting events like softball, volleyball, or tug of war.

You might not want to participate in the athletics, but you don't want to be too dressed up that you can't. Your boss and co-workers want to see how you interact outside the office. Show them your fun side and another aspect of your style.

Classic girls, you might wear a pair of tan Bermuda shorts and a fitted basic white T-shirt with flat open-toe sandals. You can still wear your diamond stud earrings, but you might want to leave the watch at home. (You don't want to look like you need to be somewhere else, and if you are going to get down and dirty on the softball field, you won't want to worry about it.) This is a completely appropriate outfit for socializing and picnicking. If you want to participate in the sports and games portion of the program, bring your running shoes, too.

Bohemian girls, your picnic outfit might consist of cutoff jean shorts, a sleeveless white peasant top, and flat gold gladiator sandals. You too might want to pack the sneakers. Rethink the jewelry. A shorter gold chain necklace won't get in the way if you're running.

Preppy girls' wardrobes are perfect for picnics. Your whole vibe is country club chic, so you are right in your element with your polo shirt, tan Bermuda shorts (or madras print, if you're in the mood), and tennis sneakers or Jack Rogers sandals.

(continued on page 188)

> Your boss and co-workers want to see how you interact outside the office. Show them your fun side and another aspect of your style.

185

CLASSIC GIRL

BOHEMIAN GIRL

PREPPY GIRL

FASHIONISTA

SURFER CHICK

SOCCER MOM

For this event you might want to don the pearl stud earrings and leave the necklace at home.

Fashionistas, you might not be used to dressing down, but we have faith you can do it, and still look fabulous. Try a pair of jean shorts with a sleeveless black top and some great black wedge sandals. Pare down the jewelry to some earrings. And, no, just because you're a girlie girl doesn't mean you can't participate. Don't forget your cool and trendy Converse sneaks.

Surfer chicks, you couldn't be happier. If only every day was the company picnic! What to choose? A tube top or tank top? Jean shorts or board shorts? Your flip-flops are totally appropriate today! Definitely bring your sneakers too, as you will probably be the first to be picked for the softball team.

Soccer moms, you too are in your comfort zone. You have had plenty of preparation for these types of activities from running around with the kids. Your tan Bermuda shorts and any of your T-shirts or tank tops would be totally appropriate for this event. Choose from your flat sandals or flip-flops, and bring sneakers. We know you will participate!

Feel free to further accessorize in any way that expresses your style. Want to add sunglasses (big black Jackie O. sunglasses for the classic girl) or a summer bag that isn't office appropriate (canvas boat tote for the preppy girl)? Go for it.

The company picnic or summer outing certainly makes for fun in the summer, and shows everyone your casual side. Now let's figure out what to wear on the other end of the spectrum.

office holiday party

Your holiday office party is the occasion to show everyone your dressed-up, sophisticated side.

Even though it's evening, it's dressy, and you're not actually in the office, the party is still a work event. Translation: Don't dress too sexy (no micro-minis or excessive cleavage) and don't get out of control!

Seriously, even though this is a party, you are still among colleagues, bosses, and clients. You still need to be professional and look the part. This doesn't mean you can't express your style. In fact, please do. And you can dress it up. So go for it.

Once again, know your audience. This comes up a lot, huh? Next to knowing yourself, knowing your audience may well be the most important consideration when picking your outfit, or anything else for that matter.

To figure out the holiday party dress code, consider where, when, and who. The venue, time and date of the party, and guest list will play a larger role than the industry in determining the fashion environment. It's likely that a big corporation will have a fancier and dressier party than a small entertainment company.

Let's assume a holiday party is at night, in a private event space, with drinks and dancing, the whole office is invited—even outside clients—and everyone is getting into the festive holiday spirit and getting dressed up. In other words: It's a cocktail party. You know what would be perfect here? Yup, your LBD! You can

absolutely wear something else if you have it, or are in the mood to buy something new, but just so you know, *you already have something to wear!* What a concept! Not only do you have the dress, but you have the metallic strappy sandals or black pumps. You have the metallic clutch and the wrap, in case you get cold or think that being a bit covered up would be more appropriate. Wow. Look at that. Your new wardrobe is working already!

To figure out the holiday party dress code, consider where, when, and who.

If you're classic, perhaps you'll choose a sleeveless crew dress that hits just above or below the knee. You might also have a structured clutch and you might choose your pumps. A bit more conservative, but that's just your style. Add your diamond studs and your watch and you'll be all set.

If you're bohemian, you might choose a flowing dress with some sort of detail or maybe a halter neckline. You will probably choose the metallic sandals and a clutch that is softer and might have beading or some other detail. Just don't go overboard with the details on both the dress and the purse. Choose one. For jewelry, put on your armful of bangles, and add some hoop earrings to dress it up.

Preppy girls, your dress might be a short-sleeve or three-quarter sleeve number that is a little on the shorter side. You might also choose the more conservative pumps over the sandals. Your clutch will have a bit more structure and a conservative slant. Your pearl necklace and earrings will be a perfect complement to your look.

Fashionista, you will have the latest in all things dress and accessories. If the trend is an asymmetric neckline, rest assured, that is the LBD you will be wearing. Your strappy sandals will be right on trend as well, most definitely a stiletto heel. Your clutch will follow suit, as it will fall under the "it" category. And, of course, so will your jewelry. Cocktail rings are all the rage? Check. You know better than to wear a necklace with an asymmetric neckline. But perhaps some fabulous earrings will do the trick.

Surfer chicks, you will prefer something soft and feminine to show off your toned frame, perhaps a spaghetti-strap dress that hits just above the knee. You might choose your metallic sandals, and you too will have a less structured clutch. Choose your chunky silver ring and perhaps your small earrings.

You soccer moms might go for a wrap dress—sexy yet elegant and appropriate. You might choose to dress it up with your sandals, and try to fit all your things into a structured metallic clutch. We know it's been a while since you've carried a purse so tiny! Add a pretty necklace to accentuate the V-neck created by the wrap, and you're complete.

In all these different style scenarios, take into account your body type and

(continued on page 194)

CLASSIC GIRL

BOHEMIAN GIRL

PREPPY GIRL

FASHIONISTA

SURFER CHICK

SOCCER MOM

what both flatters you and makes you most confident. You already will have considered fit and flatter when you bought your LBD. Great legs? Go a bit shorter. Great waist? Try a wrap, or something fitted or belted. Great arms? Strapless, sleeveless, or spaghetti strap. Want to camouflage your hips? Go for an A-line.

You get it. And, if you don't, call for reinforcement. That's why we recommend fittings with a friend. There is no occasion too small or too unimportant. If you need help, just ask! We want you to look great, feel great, have fun, and be able to say *yes* to anything and everything you want.

STEP *11*

Playing It

You have the job and the wardrobe to go with it.

What about your fun time, your down time, your *you* time? We're talking about days that you have something special to do, not just the usual gym, running errands, and ordering in.

You have your ten basic must-haves and pieces of your uniform, so let's see what your stylish self can wear to a sporting event or concert, a day out with the girls for lunch and shopping, the beach, or when traveling to your favorite vacation destination.

sporting event or concert

Let's say you are going to a big arena. You might be going to see your favorite basketball or hockey team in the play-offs, your all-time favorite band, or the hottest new artist. Either way, it's nighttime, you are in the stands with tons of people, and you are probably going to spend some time on your feet cheering, singing, dancing, or all of the above.

You need and want to look fabulous *and* functional.

You need and want to look fabulous *and* functional. Let's start with the basics. You know the arena is probably going to be air-conditioned, so you'll want to layer. You know you're going to be standing for a long period of time, so you'll want to be in comfortable shoes. You know there won't be any place to put your purse or other stuff, so you'll want to go minimalist to this event. Oh, and you want to look hot. You're a 10 no matter where you go or what you're doing.

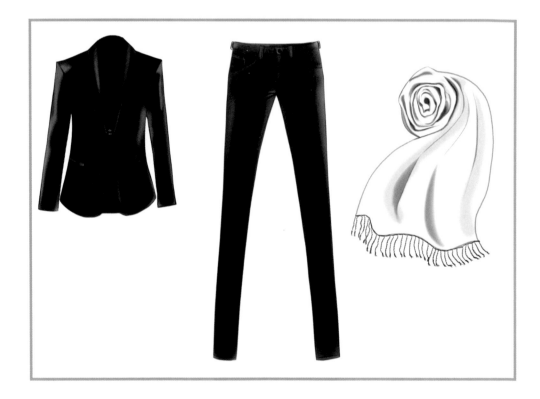

No matter what your style, we can start piecing this outfit together using the ten basic must-haves, and then personalize it with pieces of your uniform. Best of all, this outfit works whether you are going on a date or with a group of friends.

Let's see. Dark denim jeans? Check. Black blazer? Check. Wrap (which can be worn as either a wrap or a scarf). Check. The rest of the outfit (top, shoes, jewelry) will reflect your individual style.

Don't forget that these basic pieces from your must-have collection were bought to flatter *your* body type, and make you look and feel your best. In other words, like a 10.

Classic girls, true to form you will choose to wear a crisp white button-down shirt under your blazer and wrap. This is chic and sexy, and just as perfect for an evening out as for daytime.

Either flats or heels would be appropriate for this kind of activity, but we highly recommend flats. No matter what, they are always more comfortable for an evening on your feet. And flats can be dressy too. This doesn't mean sneakers. Not at all! You can wear ballet flats or even knee-high, flat riding boots. If heels are your thing, your black pumps will do the trick nicely.

What about a purse? Remember, it's just you and the chair, so there really won't be any place for your purse. Pare the items you take along to the bare minimum. Your clutch can hold them and will absolutely work with this outfit. Alternatively, try a small purse with a strap that fits across your chest so you can be hands-free all night. No worrying about holding anything or leaving anything on your chair each time you stand up. Some clutches even have chain straps that can be worn or tucked into the purse itself if you want to carry it in your hand.

Choose a thin belt to accessorize. Polish the outfit off with your diamond studs and signature leather strap watch. See how easy that was?!

CLASSIC GIRL

BOHEMIAN GIRL

PREPPY GIRL

Bohemian girls: A beautiful, soft, feminine camisole or flowing top will complement your blazer, jeans, and wrap. A top like this will soften and personalize your look.

Knowing you, you will almost always go for the flats. You welcome the opportunity to wear them whenever appropriate. Depending on the weather and your mood, you might go for the flat gold sandals, the flat knee-high boots, or ballet flats.

Opt for the small metallic clutch or purse, with an extra long strap. It might be beaded or even have some other detail—fringe, perhaps?

It's nighttime, so dress it up with jewelry. An armful of gold bangles, several layered gold chains (with charms) of different lengths, and even a pair of hoop earrings!

For you preppy girls, a lightweight crewneck sweater or top might be your choice under your blazer and wrap—totally in keeping with your vibe and style.

You are generally more at home in flats, so you're thrilled by any opportunity to wear them. You might choose a Jack Rogers sandal or perhaps a ballet flat.

Your purse might have a bit more structure to it. No matter the shape, it's available with a long enough strap. So, if you like that idea, great. If you prefer your structured metallic clutch, go for it.

For jewelry, your pearl necklace, pearl earrings, or both! This activity is in the play category, so "play" dress up.

It's nighttime, fashionistas, and you know what that means. Yes, black, black, and more black. We already knew that's what you would choose. Under your blazer and wrap, a beautiful black blouse is the perfect choice for your evening out.

We're guessing there's no way we're going to talk you out of your heels. Stilettos

FASHIONISTA

SURFER CHICK

SOCCER MOM

all the way, pain be damned. Or you might choose your metallic strappy sandals. Either way, you will be totally fashionable and totally stylish.

Your purse will be equally fabulous. Again, choose your metallic clutch or wear one with a chic long chain strap.

You're out for a fun night, so express yourself with some fun jewelry. Go for a pair of chandelier earrings plus a cocktail ring. You are definitely looking and feeling the part now. Have a blast!

Surfer chicks, you might put a vintage T-shirt under your blazer and wrap, or even an old rock concert T-shirt. You'll exude laid-back, casual style while keeping it edgy, current, and event appropriate.

You might even pair your outfit with your cool Converse sneaks. Again, totally appropriate and totally you. Don't think for a minute that this isn't sexy. It so is.

This look will accommodate the messenger bag look—wearing your purse strap across the chest. Keep it small though. You don't need much, and you're out for the evening, so let's not look like an actual messenger.

Add a pair of hanging earrings and a chunky silver ring.

Soccer moms, the V-neck top is a great option for you. Either a fitted V-neck solid T-shirt or a lightweight solid V-neck sweater will be easy and appropriate. You already have it in your arsenal, so you can be ready quickly and effortlessly. Just what you need at the end of your day!

Flats will suit you, especially because you've probably been on your feet all day. Ballet flats, sandals, or boots? Your choice.

You can stop schlepping. Mom duties are over for the evening. This night is about you. We know you are definitely going for the purse that has the messenger-

(continued on page 204)

Jill

I am a big fan of the messenger bag. (And actually of the fanny pack. Although most people think it is dorky, I think it is functional.) Whether I am going to a concert, shopping at the mall, dancing, or to a bar with friends, I always like to be hands-free. As we mentioned, there are many stylish messenger bags that will complete an outfit. The trick is to use it as an accessory. Because my favorite one has a big chain strap, I make sure my jewelry is simple so it doesn't compete with my bag. For the most part, I don't take the bag off, so I make sure my outfit is based around it rather than it being an afterthought. I am a classic girl, so my basic black blazer with jeans and white T-shirt is a perfect canvas for my fabulous bag.

Dana

A couple of summers ago, I went to the George Michael concert at Madison Square Garden in New York City. I love going to concerts. They are so much fun. Especially when you really love the artist performing. (Yes, George is one of my all-time favorites, if not favorite. And, yes, I dance and sing along.) My style being bohemian, I remember I wore my gold and brown flat open-toe sandals, jeans, and a peasant top. I brought a wrap, of course, because I don't go anywhere without it. I carried the smallest clutch I own. It is an unstructured, sort of floppy, really tiny gold metallic clutch. I was perfectly dressed for the occasion—comfortable, appropriate, in my element (free to dance and sing, and true to my style), and a happy 10. Next thing I know, I'm at the concession stand with my friend Jack getting something to drink, and who is in line right in front of us, but SJP! Yes! Sarah Jessica Parker, style icon, in sky-high stilettos! She too was wearing jeans—skinny jeans and a beautiful chic sleeveless top. Simple, sexy, very fashionista, and yet totally appropriate for the occasion. But I could not get over the heels! She was walking around the Garden in these super high stilettos! I was in awe, but she is a true fashionista after all, and the heels are the thing. At the same time, I felt reaffirmed about my own outfit and was thrilled to be in my flats!

style strap, and one that is small enough for your phone, keys, lip gloss, and nothing else.

Dress it up a bit with some jewelry. No kids grabbing at it tonight! Pick your favorite delicate necklace (to accentuate the V-neck), your wedding band, and even your engagement ring if you want to get fancy.

girls' day out

Now that we have evening activities covered, what about daytime fun? We're talking a date with your girlfriend(s) for some quality girl time. Translation: lunch and shopping.

You should get a little dressed up for these occasions. No running to brunch in your workout clothes. Look nice for yourself and your friends. Haven't you heard that girls really dress up for other girls anyway? They're the only ones who can truly appreciate your new bag or great shoes. Guys don't notice these things.

So what's the perfect daytime outfit? Well, it's funny but it's the same as the evening outfit! Give or take.

As at the concert or sporting event, you will be on your feet most of the time. That means you want to be comfortable and functional, but still look fabulous. Translation: flats. (Even you fashionistas might appreciate the value of a good pair of ballet flats on a major shopping day. You can stay on your feet longer and therefore shop longer. Isn't that what it's all about?) Pair them with jeans, a cute top, and blazer and you're good to go.

So what's the difference? Well, you'll definitely want to carry a larger purse

(still messenger style so you can shop hands-free), and you might want to tone down the jewelry (or maybe not; sometimes it's fun to wear your fancy jewelry during the day).

You can either go with the staple outfit or get creative. Let's explore the possibilities.

Classic girls, you probably won't veer too far from your uniform. It really is your comfort zone. You might trade out the white button-down for a fitted white T-shirt. You might play around with shoe options: ballet flats or flat knee-high boots. You might hold a structured purse with a short handle in your hand, or

CLASSIC GIRL

BOHEMIAN GIRL

PREPPY GIRL

carry it on your forearm, but everything else will be status quo. Classic is classic, after all.

Bohemians, you might opt for a flowing dress or peasant skirt and top instead of the jeans and blazer, but you too will otherwise remain the same. Your shoes will either be flat sandals or boots. Your jewelry will be the same. You might choose an oversize hobo bag to complement your look, but an across-the-chest strap bag will look just as good.

Preppy girls, you might trade your blazer for a cable knit sweater. You can either wear it or drape it over your shoulders. You might swap your dark denim for your white jeans. You will stick with the flats: ballet flats or Jack Rogers sandals. You might also prefer a tote with a short strap.

Fashionistas, you might choose to dress it up a bit. You are going *shopping* after all, and you want to look every bit the part when you enter your favorite boutiques. Perhaps a dress? In spite of our strong recommendation to the contrary, we know you aren't giving up the heels. Your bag will be fabulous no matter how you wear it. If you really want to mix it up, try to wear a color other than black. It is daytime, after all; show us what else is in your repertoire.

Surfer chicks, depending on the weather you might trade out your jeans and sneakers for a jean skirt and flip-flops. You might lose the blazer for a cute hoodie.

Soccer moms, you might choose a sweater instead of the blazer, but jeans and ballet flats are right up your alley. And since you are so used to carrying everything, you love the idea of a hands-free bag. Give the messenger style a try and see how freeing it is!

Again, all of these pieces are either must-haves or part of your uniform. They are the types of clothes that you will have in your personalized wardrobe.

FASHIONISTA

SURFER CHICK

SOCCER MOM

Some words of wisdom when you venture out for a day of shopping:

- No matter what your style, it's best to avoid big earrings. They get caught when you're trying on tops.
- Separates are more practical than a dress. You can take off just the top or the bottom when trying on—hence the jeans and top/blazer plan.
- We highly recommend the messenger strap bag. You can definitely find one that suits your style. They come in all shapes and sizes. It's a pleasure to have both hands free to go through the clothing racks.

day at the beach

What's more fun? In the summer or on vacation, the beach means relaxation! So don't let your outfit ruin the fun.

Of course the beach means a bathing suit, but it also means figuring out what to wear. When choosing these pieces, once again consider your body type and your style. Let's break it down.

Bathing suits can be tough to choose. They leave one totally exposed! Don't worry, there is a style to flatter every figure, and if you're still not comfortable, there is always a cover-up.

If you want to cover your tummy or back, a one-piece suit is the best choice. (There are even suits that hug you to minimize those areas.) If you are not busty, you'll look good in a triangle bikini or bandeau bikini with detail on the top. If you are busty, try a top with a bra for support, or a halter style in a dark

(continued on page 212)

Jill

I have one other rule when going shopping. Wear a great skin-tone, seamless bra, seamless underwear (I like the brand Commando), and an undergarment with control panels (Spanx all the way!). You won't be able to get an accurate appraisal of a piece without these must-have items. Here is where I get personal. I wasn't wearing a bra last week when I hit Saks. When I tried on this beautiful top, my "headlights" were showing through. I thought, "Well, when I put on a bra it will be perfect." But it wasn't. You could still see my you-know-whats. Moral of the story? Wearing the right undergarments when you shop is a must.

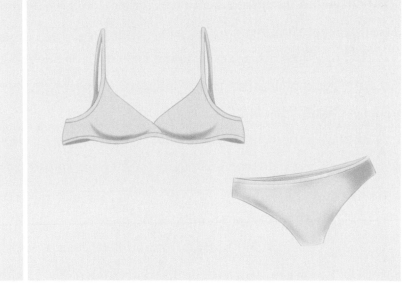

Dana

It's funny, no matter what I happen to be wearing on any given shopping day, I always end up buying something that goes with it. It's sort of strange how that happens, and it actually makes it harder to resist the purchase! I will try something on. Usually it's an accessory, because those are my favorites—a bag, shoe, or piece of jewelry—and lo and behold it works perfectly with my outfit. In fact, it makes the outfit. Every time I go to my friend Luis Morais's jewelry showroom, I leave with another bracelet. I have a small collection of bracelets that I never take off—a small gold ID bracelet from childhood, a pearl beaded one my grandmother gave me from her jewelry box, a turquoise Van Cleef & Arpels clover bracelet I got for my birthday, a coral beaded one I picked up along the way, and others. Luis's beaded bracelets with gold charms are irresistible on their own and complement the ones I already wear. I already have two and am always eyeing the next one.

The general plan for swimwear is to draw the eye to your best feature and away from whatever makes you uncomfortable. Ruffles, prints, and light colors draw attention, and solids and dark colors camouflage. Play around with what works for you and your body.

solid color. If you want your legs to appear longer, wear a suit cut higher in the leg. If you are long-waisted, a bikini will break that up. If you are short-waisted, a one-piece will elongate your look. Even though they're really cute, the boy-short bottom is tough to wear unless you're super tall and thin, in which case go for it.

The general plan for swimwear is to draw the eye to your best feature and away from whatever makes you uncomfortable. Ruffles, prints, and light colors draw attention, and solids and dark colors camouflage. Play around with what works for you and your body.

Jill

My days at the beach usually turn into drinks then somehow morph into dinner. When I leave my house to hit the sand in the morning, I plan to wear my outfit all day long (or at least know it's a possibility). There are different ways to tie a sarong to take you from day to night. I start the day with it as a skirt paired with a tank, and finish it with my sarong as a dress. I even pack earrings in my beach bag to dress up my look. Add a little lip gloss and I'm all set!

Dana

I love sarongs. They are so pretty and so functional. In my ideal life, in my head, I am living at the beach and I'm wearing them all the time. They are light and easy, and serve several purposes. I wear them over my bikinis, I use them as scarves or wraps, and I even use them to lie on at the beach. Did I mention how well they pack too? When I was in Hawaii at surf camp with my sister there were stands everywhere that sold them. Each one was prettier than the next. Beautiful colors. Beautiful prints. It was so hard to decide! I bought two. I have a small collection. They don't take up much room and they make me happy.

Regardless of your body type or style, one beachwear item will work for you: The sarong. The sarong plays a similar role as that must-have the wrap, and in fact can be used as a wrap in warmer weather. It is just as versatile and can be worn several ways. Sarongs are made of lighter, more washable material than wraps, and they come in pretty, colorful prints (and in solids, too, if you prefer).

A sarong is always chic and current. It works on every body type. It can give almost complete coverage, or less. Either way, it is sexy. Knowing you look hot and feel cool will give you the comfort and the confidence for a great day at the beach.

If you're not into sarongs or want more of an outfit, consider these other options.

Classic girls are still classic girls when they're at the beach. You will still prefer solids, and still prefer colors from your palette, such as black, navy, and white. So your bathing suit will likely be black or navy, and you might even prefer a one-piece to a bikini. So old-school and yet totally current.

If you choose a sarong, it will be solid and dark to match your bathing suit. What you might choose instead? A white button-down. Imagine that! You already own several and they look so you. You can wear the shirt buttoned or unbuttoned, tied at the waist, and by itself or paired with tan Bermuda or jean shorts.

Accessorize with a pair of flat sandals, an oversized tote bag, a pair of big black Jackie O. sunglasses, and a straw hat.

Bohemian style is very beachy, loose, and flowing to begin with. You might choose a white bathing suit or one in brown or sand. The style will of course be whatever flatters your body type.

If you choose a sarong, it will likely be white or a combination of pale browns, golds, and white, perhaps a tie-dye print. You could also opt for a loose, flowing, sheer dress or long peasant skirt in the white or natural color palette.

CLASSIC GIRL

BOHEMIAN GIRL

PREPPY GIRL

Your accessories will be thong sandals, an oversized slouchy bag, and a straw hat.

Preppy girls, you too will choose a style of swimsuit according to body type, but, true to style, you will likely choose a fun print. Polka dots, madras, even stripes? You love to experiment with color too. Pastels and brights, you like them all.

With a printed bikini, keep the sarong solid. Any of your favorite colors will do. Just make sure the color matches the bathing suit you're wearing that day. If not, your polo shirts and tan Bermuda shorts will complement nicely. And, by the way, on the beach you can wear the shirt, or the shorts, or both. Whatever makes you comfortable.

Your accessories will include your Jack Rogers sandals, a two-tone canvas boat tote, and a bucket hat.

Fashionistas, regardless of body type, might go for an elegant black one-piece bathing suit with some detail, just because it's so chic. (Only if it flatters you, of course. But really, it's hard to go wrong with a black one-piece!)

You will most likely choose the sarong because that is the epitome of beach chic. If not, you will choose a dress that looks like a sarong, because that is the "look." It might be black, or you might venture into a print if you get inspired by being out of the city and want to let go of your all-black uniform for a bit. Try it. It's only one day, and you're on holiday!

Grab your fabulous flat thong sandals (we know you have a pair), beach tote, Jackie O. sunglasses, and sun hat, and you're all set.

Surfer chicks, this is your favorite portion of the program! Most likely you will be in a sporty bikini. Being out on the waves, you want to be noticed, so likely it will be bright and have a Hawaiian print.

If you choose a bright solid, pair it with your brightly colored floral print sarong. If you don't go for the sarong, you will be in a vintage logo print tank top

FASHIONISTA

SURFER CHICK

SOCCER MOM

and jean shorts or skirt. If you're not in a rash guard, that is!

Havaianas? Check. (The flip-flops of choice for those who like to live in them.) You might even prefer a backpack for the beach. All the better to carry your stuff with your board.

Soccer moms, it's your day at the beach, with or without the kids, so express yourself. Of course find something that flatters you. Solid or print, it's up to you.

Your cover-up might be as easy as a solid sarong that works with any of your bathing suits, or it might be a T-shirt and Bermuda shorts. Whichever you prefer.

Flat sandals or flip-flops, a very big tote, and your sun hat, and you're good to go.

See, that wasn't so bad. Now you can lose the outfit worries and body image worries, and just have fun at the beach. You're a 10 and you deserve it!

planes, trains, and automobiles

A day at the beach is great, but what if you are taking a real vacation (one that requires actual luggage)?

Just because you are getting on a plane or train does not give you license to look like a slob. Yes, you may be sleeping for most of the ride, but still. A 10 is a 10 no matter when or where. You do want to be comfortable, but you also want to look put together. You never know who you'll run into at the airport, right?

Comfort means different things to everyone, so we're going to give you options for your travel outfit. A big baggy sweatsuit is not one of them.

However, you can wear a pair of leggings. Basic black leggings are both comfortable and stylish, and a pair will not break the bank. Our guess is that if you do yoga or other exercise, you probably already have a pair. (Just make sure they're not

Jill

As you know by this point, I am single. I have met so many men (and interesting people in general) while traveling. (One I actually dated for a period of time.) So I always like to dress up when I'm going on a flight. That is not to say you need to be in a black-tie dress, but you should really look your best when heading out on a trip. My uniform? I am a big fan of a cashmere sweater with a belt, black pants made of spandex so they don't wrinkle, a white T-shirt, and ballet flats. This look is chic, and comfortable, too. On a recent flight back from Los Angeles, Matthew McConaughey was sitting right next to me. I know, I know. He has a significant other (and two beautiful children) but I was still happy I was a traveling 10.

Dana

I never travel anywhere without my wrap, even for a weekend road trip in the car. It is a pale lavender pashmina (from my sister), and it matches everything. Several years ago, I went to Spain for vacation in early May. I was thinking, well, May is pretty close to summer. I'm here to tell you that it's not! Far from. But thankfully, I had my wrap. I wore that wrap over every single outfit, every day. It is in every picture I have from that trip! But you know what, that's what it's for, and that's the beauty of the basic must-haves.

the shiny, sporty looking ones. Those are only for the gym.) Again, pick a pair that flatters you. As with jeans, there are both skinny and flared leg kinds. By the way,

A 10 is a 10 no matter when or where. You do want to be comfortable, but you also want to look put together. You never know who you'll run into at the airport, right?

jeans are perfectly acceptable for travel, too, and can be substituted for the leggings in this outfit—however you are most comfortable.

Pair them with a basic white T-shirt, tank top, or long-sleeved T-shirt (depending on how warm you want to be) and a warm, open-front, belted sweater. Make sure it has no buttons to get in the way and that it hits your mid-thigh area, covering your belly, tush, and thighs.

Add ballet flats or flat boots (depending on the weather at your destination), a messenger bag (or your favorite carry-on, although free hands are a lifesaver when you're traveling), and your wrap. The wrap is crucial as it triples as a wrap, scarf, and blanket. Don't leave home without it!

This outfit works for everyone, no matter what your style or body type. The details, like your jewelry or bag, will scream "you," so don't worry that you're not expressing yourself.

It's best to keep it simple when you travel. Basics are key, as are neutral colors. This way you can mix and match this outfit with whatever's in your suitcase. The black leggings and white T-shirt are a no-brainer, as are the bag, wrap, and shoes (fashionistas, traveling in heels just looks ridiculous, especially if you end up having to run for your flight). Keep the sweater in a neutral tone as well (black, gray, or tan). You'll be happy you can wear it repeatedly. It might end up being your best friend on the trip!

So now you have your travel uniform. Consider yourself ready to play and to look good doing it.

STEP *12*

Loving It

By now we're hoping you're saying to yourself, "Wow, I *do* have something to wear!"

Putting outfits together will be easy now that you understand your style, your body type, your lifestyle, and fashion. Everything you need is right there in your gorgeously organized closet full of 10s, and life is good! (That is, if you've been dutifully following the steps. If not, it's never too late to go back and repeat a step!) Imagine, no last-minute panics, no frantic shopping, no out-of-control spending.

Believe us, we know it's fun to shop, and somehow it feels different to wear something new. We want you to have fun with your clothing. We want you to enjoy the process of building a wardrobe and getting dressed both every day and for special occasions. What we don't want you to feel is pressure and frustration.

You know what happens when you get the outfit portion of your life under control, don't you? Yes! You get to enjoy the rest of it.

Now that you know how to work it and play it, let's find out how to love it. Our favorite part!

first date

Ah, the first date. So full of excitement and promise and possibilities! (We're going to assume you're excited about it, even if it's a blind date. Plenty of fairy-tale stories started this way!)

Whether this is your first time around, or you've been married before and are looking for love again, a first date is a first date. The same rules apply. You want to be confident, show your personality, show your style, be sexy but not too exposed, and dress up without looking like you're trying too hard. Basically, show off your best self. Just like in a job interview, get the offer first, then decide if you want it!

We are also going to assume that this date is for either drinks or dinner or, if it goes well, both. If he's really bold, and he takes you to a concert, show, or sporting event, well, the same outfit will work with a little tweaking. You're already a pro at getting dressed for a fun evening out. So, no matter what your age or your style, here's the rundown.

> You want to be confident, show your personality, show your style, be sexy but not too exposed, and dress up without looking like you're trying too hard.

Start with dark denim jeans and your black blazer (they both fit you perfectly, obviously). Next add a top. Choose one that is so you, so your style, and so comfortable that you might take off your blazer mid-date if all goes well (or if it's just hot)! Maybe it's sexier than the one you would wear to a concert with your girlfriends.

Maybe it's dressier. Maybe it's the same one. Just make sure you're not worried about it (meaning you don't need double-stick tape or anything else to keep it in place). First dates are nerve-wracking enough. There's no need to add the possibility of wardrobe malfunction.

This is a date, so we highly recommend heels. They are way sexier, and chances are good that you will be sitting most of the time anyway, so really go for it.

Jill

My first date outfit (unless I am being whisked away to Paris, which hasn't happened yet) is always the same. It is the "I-am-not-trying" look. Jeans are a definite. And I usually wear a tight T-shirt with a black blazer over it. I also opt for heels when first meeting someone. I like someone who is taller than me when I'm in heels, so I may as well get that test over with. I wear one fun piece of jewelry, but nothing too showy. I think you should always be who you are, but overdoing it on a first date could come off as intimidating, even a little ridiculous, depending on your destination.

Dana

The thing that's so great about a first date is that it's the first one. That means even if I've worn the same outfit time and again, he is never the wiser. So I do. There's no need to stress about what to wear on a first date. Who knows? It could be the first *and* the last. My philosophy: If it ain't broke, don't fix it.

Depending on how dressy you want to get, you can choose from your black pumps, strappy metallic sandals, or even boots. It's your call, but heels really do show that you made an effort (not to mention that they will boost your confidence because you know you look hot).

Either your metallic clutch or your black midsize purse would be appropriate. However, *do not* schlep your oversized work bag. You want to look fresh and together, not frazzled, rushed, and distracted from a day at work.

Absolutely wear a piece of dressy or fun jewelry, but don't overdo it. He's there to meet you, see you, and get to know you. Too much going on in the jewelry department can get distracting, and that's certainly not what you want. Here's a good trick when accessorizing: Put on everything you want to wear, stand with your back to a mirror, turn around quickly, and take off whatever catches your eye. That's the piece that is too much. Or just pick one great accent piece and call it a day.

We guess there are no more excuses about why you won't go on that date!

meeting his parents

You find yourself in an actual relationship. Fancy that! It's going so well, in fact, that he just asked you to meet his parents! Yes, well, that's what happens when you put yourself together, make a little effort, get out of the house, and show the world your perfect 10 self.

Don't panic. We've got you covered. By now, your boyfriend has seen you in not only your first date outfit but many others. Part of what he loves about you is your style. It's an expression of your personality, after all. When you meet his parents, feel free to keep expressing yourself, carefully and cautiously at first, respectfully always. Nevertheless, show them who you are.

You can wear either something similar to your first date outfit (it worked on their son!) or something else from your repertoire. You can choose the blazer and jeans option, and even the purse and jewelry can be the same, but let's discuss the top and shoes. You took it up a notch in the sexy/dressy category for the date, but to meet the parents for the first time, take it down a notch—more like your job interview outfit. Pick a top that is *you*, just the less sexy version. A great classic staple that is always appropriate, no matter what your style and no matter what the occasion, is the white button-down shirt. You can still wear heels, but the pumps might be more appropriate. This outfit works whether you are meeting them for Sunday brunch or Friday night dinner.

> When you meet his parents, feel free to keep expressing yourself, carefully and cautiously at first, respectfully always. Nevertheless, show them who you are.

If you decide to express yourself even further (sort of like your first day at work, after you already have the job) by all means do. Take the activity into account, but we're going with the assumption that this meeting will be taking place around a meal. That means you should plan an outfit that's not too dressy but totally put together.

As always, know your audience. We can't stress this enough. Your boyfriend has probably filled you in on most of the details that you'll need to figure out what's appropriate to wear (and say). If they're conservative, it's no skin off your back to dress a little more conservatively. If they're a bit more relaxed and free-spirited, then you have a little more wiggle room. If things go well, you will have plenty of opportunity to express yourself around them, so for the first meeting pick what you're sure is going to be a hit.

Classic girls, you will likely choose the jeans and blazer option, but if you want to dress it up, or are just in the mood to wear a skirt, you might choose your black skirt and white button-down shirt with black pumps and a structured black purse. Add your signature jewelry pieces and you will be classically perfect.

Bohemians, you might pick an outfit that is more flowing and feminine. Perhaps a pretty dress and flat boots or gold sandals. Pair with a hobo style bag and beautiful bangles. You will be perfectly appropriate and totally bohemian.

Preppies, you might opt for something more casual, more *you*. Your white jeans and cable knit sweater will do the trick. Pair them with your ballet flats or Jack Rogers sandals, pearls, and a medium-sized, light color purse and you will look the part.

Fashionistas, we're guessing that you like the dark denim and blazer option paired with a chic blouse, but if you want to change it up, you might opt for a chic black dress. Either way, you'll choose your stiletto pumps and whichever purse strikes your mood, the metallic clutch or the black purse. Add one piece of statement jewelry and you are confident and ready.

Surfer chicks, you might show your true colors by trading the jeans for a jean skirt. Paired with a soft, feminine tank and your black blazer, you can show off your sporty side. Either flat sandals (no flip-flops please) or boots will work with this outfit. Add a chunky silver ring and you are in your element.

Soccer moms, you've probably been down this road before. But we know it's no less nerve-wracking. That's OK. You've got it under control. You're chic and confident in your beautiful black wrap dress, which your black pumps will perfectly complement. A pretty necklace to accentuate the neckline of your dress will polish you off to perfection.

CLASSIC GIRL

BOHEMIAN GIRL

PREPPY GIRL

FASHIONISTA

SURFER CHICK

SOCCER MOM

weddings

Not yours, silly. One may be in your future, but that's another book entirely.

You have been invited to a wedding. What's more celebratory than two people embarking on an adventure together? This is your opportunity to celebrate, party, and share your love with the happy couple. Whether you are attending with a date or flying solo, it's hard not to enjoy yourself at these affairs. Especially when you look amazing and didn't have to spend a dime! Of course, we know you sometimes want to buy something new (especially if it's a beach destination wedding, and you are going on a little holiday), but, just so you know, your LBD is totally appropriate.

Remember back in step 8 where we discussed old fashion rules? Wedding

This is your opportunity to celebrate, party, and share your love with the happy couple. Whether you are attending with a date or are flying solo, it's hard not to enjoy yourself at these affairs. Especially when you look amazing and didn't have to spend a dime!

attire has evolved, too, and the old ideals about dress length have gone by the wayside. Especially if your LBD is above the knee and if the wedding is on a Saturday night, chances are good that you can wear it. (Unless, which is rare, floor-length gowns are expected.) And the old myth about not wearing black at a wedding is long gone.

This will be a fun wedding with lots of music, dancing, socializing, and you looking fabulous. Let's start with

(continued on page 236)

Loving It

233

Jill

Because of my job I am often photographed when I go to events. Some people gasp at the thought of wearing the same thing you have worn before, but I am not in that camp. I think when you love something you should wear it again, but as Dana will explain next, it is best to break it out for different groups of people in different situations. When I was in Italy with my parents, I bought this beautiful backless lace dress. I love it not only for the way it looks, but also because I bought it with my mother, and every time I wear it I think of our vacation. I have already worn it three times: once with bangles, once with big earrings, and once with flip-flops. All looks were different, but all were fabulous. And it will totally work for a wedding, too. Just by switching the accessories, I feel like I have an entirely new outfit each time I put it on. This is real life, not *Sex and the City*. There's nothing wrong with repeating outfits in different ways!

Dana

I have a dress—it's not black, it's yellow, in fact—that I have worn to three weddings, one birthday dinner, and one family holiday. And I will wear it again. It is short (mini in fact), and three-quarter sleeve. I wore it to back-to-back weddings (both fancy and at night)—first in Santa Barbara at a gorgeous ranch, and then again the very next weekend at an elegant hotel wedding in New York City. Both times I wore my strappy gold sandals, gold metallic clutch, and lavender pashmina wrap. There were two entirely separate groups of friends and no one was the wiser. I was traveling from Miami, so I had to pack only one dress. Brilliant! I then wore it the following year to yet another fancy, evening wedding (with an entirely different group) at a beautiful waterfront estate in Miami. I even wore the same accessories, only this time, I went so far as to wear flats. Yes! Flats! Dressy gold flats, but still flats. We danced all night, and I was the most comfortable one there, and the most chic, if I may say so myself. The birthday dinner was a different group, and the family holiday was a different audience. Aside from the pictures, no one would know how often I've worn that dress! I've certainly had my money's worth and then some. By the way, that dress is not over. It is current, fits me perfectly, and is totally my style. Even at these three very fancy weddings, at entirely differ-ent locations and venues, I got away with the short dress, and saved myself a fortune!

what we already know. Your LBD is a 10. It is the perfect cut for your body and it is the perfect style for you. Even a black dress can express your personality. Don't underestimate the power of the LBD!

No one will know this is the same dress you wore to your office's holiday party. The crowd will be completely different. The beauty of a little black dress is you can wear it time and again, and no one will be able to remember!

Break yours out. Dress it up with your strappy metallic high heeled sandals, your metallic clutch, your wrap, and your jewels. See how easy that was? Now go have fun!

sexy at home

What happens at the end of the night? That's right. Eventually, it's time to go home.

Whether you are with someone or alone, you know the rule: 10 only. Even loungewear and sleepwear. Being a 10 is a mental game as much as anything else. If you feel sexy, you are sexy. So let's get you wearing things that make you feel that way.

Like underwear, what you wear in bed or around the house is less about your personal style (classic, bohemian, preppy, etc.) than about what makes you comfortable. But oversize, baggy, ripped, or stained sweatsuits need not apply.

Ready for bed? Perhaps you feel best in sexy lingerie. Cute, fitted pajama set? Either way, every item must fulfill the criteria of what it means to be a 10. If none of your sleepwear made the cut when you did your rounds, it's time to replenish. Here's an opportunity to take a look at what you want to express to your partner, or what you want to feel like when you walk past the mirror, even on a night in on your own.

Being a 10 is a mental game as much as anything else. If you feel sexy, you are sexy. So let's get you wearing things that make you feel that way.

You know what else works at home? Your leggings and fitted T-shirts. Your airplane outfit does double duty at home. (And if you're traveling, you'll be glad to lounge in it at the hotel.)

Want to know what's most classic and sexy of all? You all own one. It's the white button-down shirt! On its own with nothing else. It works for lounging at home and in the bedroom. And, no, you don't have to be a classic girl to wear this. It's chic, sexy, and functional.

In the safe haven of your home, feel free to experiment with what makes you feel sexy and special, as long as it fits and flatters you and is in perfect condition. You might feel braver at home to try bolder colors or sheer fabrics, or you might still be your conservative self. Either way, find what works for you and make it part of your uniform. We are all creatures of habit. You know you always grab for the same pieces anyway, so own only those.

the moral of the story

Whether you're dressing for work, play, or love, wear what makes you feel most confident and most like *you*.

As you continue to build your wardrobe, consider the styles to be guidelines, not absolutes. You might be a hybrid of two styles, possibly three. Maybe you're a classic girl who wants to experiment with statement jewelry. Go for it! If you're preppy and you want to change it up and wear something trendy and edgy, by all means do. If you are a soccer mom who is a closet fashionista, work it.

Styles aside, you want to buy only what you are actually going to wear. When

Jill

I make sure I feel sexy when my day is over. It is nice to do something for yourself and feel like you are at your best even when you are solo. My uniform? Hanky Panky lace boy shorts and a very soft white tank. I just feel better when getting into bed. If I am seeing someone, I turn things up a notch, but that is for a non-PG book!

Dana

I always look cute at home. Yes, even when I'm alone. *Always.* There is no reason to own anything that does not make me feel and look great, at home or out on the town. No exceptions. I love white, as I've mentioned, so most of my loungewear is white. I have a supply of white tanks and white boy shorts. This is my lounge/sleep outfit of choice. Of course, I have a supply of lingerie for those occasions that warrant it, and a couple pairs of cute, fitted sweatpants for the winter months, but that's pretty much how you'll find me at home. Sexy, comfy, and totally me.

you understand who you are and what you are trying to express, your style will shine through. Once you have a handle on your style, anything you buy should work with all of the other pieces in your closet. Just be true to yourself. You'll be able to mix and match most of your pieces.

> Once you have a handle on your style, anything you buy should work with all of the other pieces in your closet. Just be true to yourself. You'll be able to mix and match most of your pieces.

Did you catch that you can wear the same thing to a job interview, sporting event, and first date, with a little tweaking and some accessories? Likewise, you can wear the same incarnation of your uniform to the first day at a new job, to lunch and shopping with the girls, and to meet his parents. Again, a little tweaking is involved, but the basic idea is the same.

Along those lines, the company picnic and a day at the beach have similar elements. So do the office holiday party and weddings. Your loungewear will have overlap. The same T-shirt and leggings you wear on the plane can be your at-home loungewear.

In fact, you can get to any activity in your life with just five outfits! Break it down and see.

So there you have it. We have outlined the steps and taught you what we know. You're ready to go out on your own. Don't worry. You have the tools and know-how. You know who you are. You have a beautiful, clean, and organized closet. You have given back to help others. You understand modern fashion and your body type. You know your style, and have a "uniform" to express it. You are armed with the ten basic wardrobe must-haves. All of your clothes are 10s. And so are you. So get out there. Work it, play it, and love it with everything you have, because your wardrobe is not going to hold you back ever again.

If you need us, we'll be here. Come back to the book whenever you need a refresher or a reality check. We'll be happy to be your sponsor anytime!

You're ready to go out on your own. Don't worry. You have the tools and know-how. You know who you are. You have a beautiful, clean, and organized closet.

Definitions

How we define our favorite words.

10: The highest score on a scale (1 to 10) used to grade the items in your wardrobe when you are deciding what to keep, get rid of, or purchase new. If it's not a 10, it is unacceptable to keep or buy.

Fitting: Trying on clothing, with your friend, sponsor, or by yourself to find the perfect outfit for a specific occasion or even to pack for a trip.

Hoarding: Holding on to unnecessary clothing items for no apparent reason.

Must-Have: A basic clothing item that everyone must have in her closet. There are ten that we think are essential.

Round: Going through your closet, with your sponsor or on your own, deciding what makes the cut and what to get rid of.

Sharing: Our confessions to you about where we've gone wrong and right on our fashion journeys, and the lessons we've learned about making our wardrobes work for us.

Sponsor: Trusted friend or relative with a keen eye and an honest tongue, to hold your hand through the closet clean-out process.

Uniform: The outfit that you gravitate toward most often on a daily basis. The one that expresses your style and your personality, and best suits your lifestyle. Your closet should be filled with items that comprise your uniform rather than random pieces of different styles that aren't you and never get worn.

Acknowledgments

The authors wish to thank the following people for all of their support, advice, guidance, participation, and expertise…

The amazing and creative editing, design, and marketing team at Rodale: Shannon Welch, Nancy Bailey, Kara Plikaitis, Wendy Gable, Amy King, Olivia Baniuszewicz, Aly Mostel, Marie Crousillat, and Stephanie Knapp.

The knowledgeable and invaluable team at WME: Mel Berger, Strand Conover, Mark Mullett, Henry Reisch, and Scott Wachs.

The ever-important and incredible beauty team: Eric Striffler, Todd Plitt, Alyssa Shackil, and Petula Skeete.

The generous and fashionable Kathie Lee Gifford, Hoda Kotb, and Amar'e Stoudemire.

And a special thank you to Pierre Lehu.

Thank you, thank you, thank you!